Praise for the *NVC Companion Workbook*:

"It amazes me how much we actually covered in class time using the *NVC Companion Workbook*. We went over real-life situations and followed various exercises that promoted understanding the content more fully. Practicing with this workbook was the key for my success in understanding and using NVC!"

—Kirsten Ingram, finance and administration officer, Children's Commission Province of British Columbia, Canada

"I was recently contracted by the BC government to facilitate NVC practice sessions for three different groups of government staff. I feel immense gratitude for the *NVC Companion Workbook* and the support it provided me in sharing the Nonviolent Communication process during the thirteen sessions I offered each group. Clear, concise, fun, and supportive, the workbook exercises and reading reviews provide tremendous tools to integrate NVC into everyday life, at work, at home, and at play."

—Penny Wassman, certified NVC trainer, Victoria, BC, Canada

"The *NVC Companion Workbook* draws out the essential NVC elements in a way that is fun to practice and makes learning the material much easier."

—Jeff Carl, author of *Relationship Intelligence: Select and Nurture Healthy Relationships*

"The *NVC Companion Workbook* provides a comprehensive, turnkey program for people of any experience level to lead a group in practicing Nonviolent Communication. As the perfect companion to *Nonviolent Communication: A Language of Life*, the workbook provides universally applicable activities to reinforce your learning."

—Stuart Watson, facilitator and mediator, Portland, OR, USA

"I have used this workbook now in two prison facilities. It has been a wonderful tool for men and women who are committed to gaining useful life skills in some of the toughest of environments."

—Karen M Campbell, workforce/lifeskills coordinator, Coffee Creek Corrections Facility, Salem, OR, USA

Working weekly with three different practice groups, it's been my experience that members with their own copy of the *NVC Companion Workbook* progress to 'living' the practice of NVC faster than those who don't. Lucy Leu's workbook promotes practice, lively discussion, and a deepening of NVC consciousness. My only wish would be to see it available in all bookstores, right next to Marshall Rosenberg's book.

—M.F., Victoria, BC, Canada

"In my opinion this Workbook is a very valuable resource for people who are self-directed learners and wish to continue their study of NVC. I will be recommending it to my 220 students. I have also included Rosenberg's *Nonviolent Communication: A Language of Life* as recommended reading for communication students."

—C.C.M., USA

"The *NVC Companion Workbook* allows people—without even a smattering of knowledge about NVC—to effectively learn and practice the process. I would not be facilitating study groups if it were not for this workbook. It contains questions to check reading comprehension, group exercise options that can be used or modified as the study group facilitator sees fit, and essential tools like the feelings and needs lists to build your emotional vocabulary. Would I recommend it? You bet . . . highly!"

—T.M., Portland, Oregon, USA

"THANK YOU again, Lucy, for writing this workbook—it really makes my life more wonderful!!!"

—K.B., Denmark

"My two practice groups have found your *NVC Companion Workbook* to be so useful! The questions you posed in your Taking Time section is my favorite part—I've mounted the questions on large flashcards, which we keep available during our practice sessions. When I think of the time Lucy took to develop the exercises and thought-provoking questions, and to integrate all this with each part of Marshall's book, I'm awed and so very grateful. The manual helps me get even more depth, understanding, and proficiency in the NVC approach, which is creating such profound transformation in how I experience and participate in life."

—L.R., Bellevue, WA, USA

"Although the basic model of NVC is quite simple, the practice and understanding of connecting at the heart seems to be a continual learning process. We especially appreciate the opportunity to become aware of our habitual patterns—enabling more conscious choices—each time we participate in the practice of NVC during the 13-week course using Lucy Leu's *NVC Companion Workbook*."

—J.M., Albuquerque, NM, USA

"The *NVC Companion Workbook* has been invaluable to me. As a new practice facilitator, the three sections for each chapter (Individual Assignments, Leader's Guide, and Sample Responses) offer a helpful balance of homework, opportunities to share from the homework, and opportunities to move on into exercises initiated by the leader. I also appreciate the reminders to launch out the discussion from the group's responses. With this workbook I've moved to deeper connections with those around me."

—S.M., USA

"I have had the pleasure of using Lucy Leu's *NVC Companion Workbook* in group practice sessions since September 2001. I would go home after each practice group I was leading, saying out loud 'Thank you, Lucy Leu'. I felt happy and confident; my need for support and reassurance was met."

—K.K., Søndersø, Denmark

Nonviolent
COMMUNICATION™
Companion Workbook

A Practical Guide for Individual, Group, or Classroom Study

by Lucy Leu

Certified Trainer
Center for Nonviolent Communication (CNVC)

PuddleDancer
P R E S S

P.O. Box 231129, Encinitas, CA 92023-1129
email@PuddleDancer.com • www.PuddleDancer.com

Nonviolent Communication Companion Workbook:
A Practical Guide for Individual, Group, or Classroom Study
By Lucy Leu, Certified Trainer for the
Center for Nonviolent Communication (CNVC)
Copyright © 2003 Center for Nonviolent Communication
A PuddleDancer Press Book

PuddleDancer Press, Permissions Dept.
P.O. Box 231129, Encinitas, CA 92023-1129
Fax: 1-858-759-6967

All feedback is welcome. Please direct comments to:
Lucy Leu, c/o PuddleDancer Press at the address above or in care of
Freedom_Project@hotmail.com

Nonviolent Communication Companion Workbook:
A Practical Guide for Individual, Group or Classroom Study

1st Edition Printing August, 2003

Author: Lucy Leu

Editors: Liv Monroe, Garry Simpson, Peter Vennewitz,
        Peter Weismiller, Graham Van Dixhorn, Rita Herzog

Cover and interior design: Lightbourne LLC, www.lightbourne.com

Cover photograph of Jeruselem artichoke: Eric Dresser

Manufactured in the United States of America

10 9 8 7 6 5

ISBN: 1-892005-04-2

Contents

Appendices • 169

Preface

This workbook is designed to be used in conjunction with Marshall B. Rosenberg's book, *Nonviolent Communication: A Language of Life* (formerly titled *Nonviolent Communication: A Language of Compassion,* Puddledancer Press). It provides a 13-week curriculum for the practice of Nonviolent Communication (NVC). It is suggested that readers familiarize themselves with Marshall's book before beginning this workbook.

A Note on Giraffes and Jackals

In many countries Nonviolent Communication is popularly known as "Giraffe Language." Marshall picked the giraffe, the land animal with the largest heart, as a symbol for NVC, a language that inspires compassion and joyful relationships in all areas of life. Like NVC, the giraffe's height affords a long view into the distance and provides a heightened awareness of future possibilities and the consequences of our thoughts, words, and actions. As a language that stresses the expression of feelings and needs, NVC invites vulnerability and transforms it into strength. The long neck of the giraffe reminds us of this important quality of vulnerability.

In some countries, Marshall uses a jackal puppet to represent that part of ourselves that thinks, speaks, or acts in ways that disconnect us from our awareness of our own feelings and needs, as well as the feelings and needs of others. The word "giraffe" is sometimes used interchangeably with NVC, and may also refer to a practitioner of NVC. Within the context of "giraffe" and "jackal," a jackal is simply a giraffe with a language problem. As a friend, the jackal gives us the message that we are unlikely to get our needs met if we continue as we are. Just as the pain of a burn is our friend because it reminds us to remove our hand from the hot stove, the jackal reminds us to take our time and find the giraffe way to hear and think before we speak. The NVC practice is to recognize and befriend our "jackals" by welcoming them into awareness and allowing them to lead us to our feelings and needs. Doing so as compassionately and as free from moral judgment as we are able, we experience life in ever more fulfilling ways.

For many, the use of puppets helps to distinguish these two parts of ourselves (or these two ways of thinking and speaking) and is an effective learning aid that brings clarity and play into the practice of NVC.

Please note: The Center for Nonviolent Communication's use of the image and term "giraffe" is in no way connected to The Giraffe Project, a completely separate organization producing its own trainings and educational materials. Also, in some countries, NVC trainers use animals other than the giraffe and jackal. In English, "Giraffe Language," "Compassionate Communication," and "NVC" are synonymous with "Nonviolent Communication."

In former printings of this manual, the words "giraffe" and "jackal" were used throughout the text. Because of the workbook's widening use around the world, and the fact that these two terms are not easily translated—or not translatable at all—in the remainder of the book these terms have been replaced with literal descriptions.

Acknowledgments

The assignments in this workbook were originally inspired by and created for people who were incarcerated, isolated from training resources, and who were intent on practicing NVC behind bars. Later the assignments were incorporated into a manual to support "leaderful" practice groups in the general community—groups devoted to practicing NVC on their own without a trainer or single leader.

I wish to express my appreciation to Marshall Rosenberg for bringing NVC to life and for the encouragement and confidence he has offered me over many years. In my growth as an NVC practitioner, I am particularly indebted and grateful to my son Felix, my husband Peter, and to fellow Giraffes of the Puget Sound who offer the gem of living and working in Giraffe community.

PART I

Using this Workbook

Using this Workbook

Purpose of this Workbook

This workbook is designed for use with Marshall B. Rosenberg's book *Nonviolent Communication: A Language of Life*. It is intended for:

1. Persons new to Nonviolent Communication who seek a comprehensive curriculum in order to learn and apply the basic principles of NVC, either on their own or in a group setting. NVC requires the development of new habits of thought and speech. However impressed we may be by NVC concepts, it is only through practice and application that our lives will be transformed. This curriculum supports the reader through thirteen weeks of learning and ongoing practice, either as an individual or in a group experience. It also offers the possibility of thirteen months of dedicated practice. The practice suggested for a week is practiced instead for a month. Those who use the workbook at this next level of commitment will enjoy an ever-deepening fluency and capacity for connection.

2. Persons wishing to engage in regular group practice. This manual offers:

   - guidance in starting a practice group

   - content and structure for 13 sessions

   - suggestions for forming a "leaderful practice circle," and activities for ongoing groups

   - support in identifying and addressing challenges often encountered by NVC practice groups.

3. Persons whose own lives have been touched by NVC and who are drawn to pass on the gift. Group leaders and teachers may use this curriculum as a springboard from which to develop their own courses.

Please note that the group practice and activity sections of this edition of the workbook have been modified to assist individual practice. These places are indicated by use of the ◎ symbol.

Suggestions for Use of this Workbook

There are thirteen assignments in this curriculum that correlate with the thirteen chapters of Marshall B. Rosenberg's book, *Nonviolent Communication: A Language of Life*, which offers a comprehensive teaching of Nonviolent Communication basics. Consider completing a chapter each week: this provides regularity and gives enough time to absorb new material, but not so much time as to forget what was learned earlier.

Please note that in this workbook, the words "Marshall" and "the book" refer to Marshall B. Rosenberg and his book, Nonviolent Communication: A Language of Life. Because the several editions of the book do not share the same number of chapters or page numbering, reference in this workbook to a specific part of the book is made by identifying chapter and subheading rather than page number.

1. First read a chapter of the book.

2. Go to the corresponding individual assignment in Part IV of this workbook. Each assignment consists of two parts:

   "Reading Review" is a set of straightforward questions on the contents of the chapter that you may use to review or to recall what you have read. Most readers wait until they finish reading the chapter and use the questions as a way to test themselves and jog their memory on what they've learned. Others respond to the questions while they are reading so as to focus and to remember the contents better. You can experiment using (or not using) them in a way that best supports your learning.

   "Individual Practice" consists of exercises and activities for applying what you have read. It may include self-observation, reflection, practice, and role-play. Most may be completed on the spot, but a few require time over the course of a week. When you finish an assignment, you may want to quickly check the following week's assignment for any activity that may require a series of days to complete.

Note to Individuals and Group Members: It will be helpful to keep a notebook or computer handy to record your responses to the exercises, as well as any ideas, feelings, and needs that occur to you in the course of your study.

3. If you are practicing with a group, you will be covering the exercises given in the Leader's Guides when you meet together. Before you begin, read Sections A-F in Part III (Practicing Together) about setting up a group, developing a structure, remembering our purpose, leading the circle, rules, and feedback. Read the other Sections (G-K) as the respective subjects arise during the course of your 13-week practice. These sections cover subjects that may arise and offer some ideas about how to stay connected to the spirit of the NVC process while resolving what may appear as conflicted needs within the group.

4. If you are practicing alone, look over the Leader's Guide and Sample Responses corresponding to the chapter and assignment you just completed. These exercises and activities are easily adapted for individual use and examples of what you might do are included. After completing the exercise you might like to examine the Sample Responses that follow the Leader's Guide for each chapter.

PART II

Practicing Alone

Practicing Alone

In learning NVC, as with learning a foreign language, we first need to grasp the concepts—learn the grammar, so to speak—and then to practice on a regular basis. Fortunately, unlike foreign languages, NVC can be practiced anywhere and with anybody. We do not need an NVC partner to practice: we can practice when we cash a check at the bank, when another market researcher on the phone interrupts our dinner, when we listen to campaign speeches on TV, when the police officer stops us . . . We can practice with our parents and children, co-workers and bosses, friends, lovers, strangers, enemies, and—most importantly—with ourselves.

The challenge for most of us living busy lives is to commit time and energy and then to follow through. This workbook provides contents to help you structure a 13-week course to initiate your practice of NVC. After completion of the readings and assignments, you will hopefully feel confident in your understanding of NVC concepts and be familiar enough with practice approaches to be able to develop and maintain an individualized program of practice.

When committing to a course of study or practice on your own, it is helpful to be clear about how you hope to benefit, the commitments you are willing to make, the amount of time you will invest, and the regularity of your practice. As an individual embarking on a 13-week study period, spending time clarifying your goals and committing to specific times of practice can help ensure success. Writing down your goals and commitments to practice and reviewing your progress regularly may, in some measure, replace the encouragement you would receive through group practice, where others are there to support you in keeping your commitments. Many individuals have successfully used this workbook to develop deeper understanding of NVC concepts and greater fluency in their application, resulting in an increased capacity to relate to themselves and others with empathy and honesty.

Part IV of the workbook has three components: Individual Assignments, Leader's Guides, and Sample Responses.

Individual Assignments—these consist of a "Reading Review" exercise and an "Individual Practice" exercise. Each of these exercises may be used by an individual as well as for group learning.

Leader's Guides and Sample Responses—although designed for group experience, these sections are easily adapted for individual use. Throughout these sections we have included notes accompanied by the symbol ◉ to help you as an individual work through them on your own. Additionally, once you have read the instructions for each activity, pause to listen to the "internal dialogue" that follows.

In order to take maximum advantage of the exercises in this workbook, consider establishing and staying committed to a scheduled routine. Sometimes the best of intentions are sidetracked by a schedule so flexible that it is no schedule at all. You might also wish to:

- Create a physical space dedicated to your practice of NVC. Select an area that affords whatever level of quiet and order you need to stay focused on the exercises you are committed to doing in your daily or weekly practice. You may want to find a place outdoors where you feel particularly peaceful and aware. Or, make a special place in a part of your living space where you keep items such as poems, pictures, or candles—anything that helps keep you in touch with that creative and passionate part of you that is motivated to do this work.

- Keep paper, an audio recorder, or computer "notepad" with you every day as you interact in your world. From time to time, take a moment to jot down a few words that act as mental bookmarks and serve to remind you of any thoughts or interactions you want to consider at a later time.

PART III

Practicing Together

Practicing Together

A—Creating a Practice Group

When joining or creating a group, it is helpful to be clear about what you hope to gain and what you are willing to give. While most NVC practice groups serve several purposes, one group might agree to focus on developing fluency in using the process while another might emphasize the sense of community inspired by the spirit of NVC. Likewise, one person may want to invest limited time and emotional energy, while another values the group as a major commitment in their life. Such differences can be reconciled and are less likely to lead to confusion and conflict if, individually and collectively, members can bring clarity and honest disclosure of needs in relation to their expectations.

The following are common motivations for joining a practice group:

- To learn or review NVC concepts

- To develop fluency in using the process

- To gain support in one's practice and commitment by belonging to a like-minded community

- To meet needs for empathy and connection

- To develop friendships that are grounded in NVC

- To be inspired and reminded of NVC purpose and consciousness

- To serve life and contribute to the community by sharing NVC through teaching or leadership skills

One way for a single person to generate a practice group is to bring together some people to watch an NVC video such as Marshall Rosenberg's "Making Life Wonderful" (See *Appendix 8. Further Resources*). Tell the group what's behind your own interest in NVC and in starting a group. Introduce the book and workbook as resources for a group to teach themselves the skills demonstrated in the video.

There are as many ways to structure a practice group as there are those who wish to cultivate and practice NVC consciousness. Suggestions are given here and in the Leader's Guides to assist you in experimenting with structure. A willingness to deviate from "the way we have always done it in the past" may increase the likelihood of more fully meeting the individual and collective needs of your particular group. Remember that by embracing discussions and disagreements about structure you are each affirming your choice to practice the process. Some groups have used this process as a major source of learning while also recognizing that the further along a group is in staying connected to the principles of NVC and mastering NVC skills, the greater the group's capacity to co-create a mutually enjoyable outcome.

To match the curriculum of this workbook, consider forming a group of 5-8 members to meet weekly for two-and-a-half hours over the course of at least 13 weeks.* You may want to organize a preliminary meeting for people to get to know each other and to agree on basic structure, procedures, and the materials (book and workbook) to be used. At this first meeting, it may be useful to review together *Part I: Using this Workbook*, and sections A-F of *Part III: Practicing Together*.

---

*Note: 21 weeks is a more preferable length since it allows another 8 weeks of practice after the group has completed the basic curriculum. Please note that there have been successful groups that have been as large as 12, as small as four, have met biweekly, or only for two hours each time.

A recommended structure to accompany the use of this workbook is the "leaderful practice circle." The circle evokes inclusiveness, balanced participation, and community. Leadership may be rotated so that each member has an opportunity to contribute and to practice facilitating, teaching, and guiding the circle. All members are leaders in that they all take responsibility for the well-being of the circle. The tasks of defining and realizing the purpose, nature, and direction of the circle belong to everyone.

In communities where NVC trainers are available, leaderful circles can benefit by inviting trainers to lead specific parts of the meetings. In this way, members continue to "own" the circle and to rotate overall leadership while being called to practice the art of making clear requests to their guest mentors.

B—Remembering our Purpose and Taking Time

By choosing community as our crucible for learning, we are opening ourselves not only to the beauty and power of human connections, but also to the pain of unmet needs triggered by our interactions with each other. To fully appreciate both the joys and the hurts, and to grow from them throughout your time with each other, try to:

1. Find ways to remember the purpose of being together.

For example, you might clearly demarcate the time and space you share by:

    a. opening and closing each gathering consciously with a reading, candle, music, story, silence, bell, etc.

    b. creating a "centerpiece" (with a picture, flower, poem, etc.) as a reminder of that place of infinite compassion in each of us, a place where there is no separation of "me" and "them."

You might also create frequent opportunities for the expression of appreciation (for yourself, life, others, each other, the group, etc.) and for celebration (of miracles and successes, big and small).

⏻ REMEMBER TO TAKE TIME!

2. Take time.

We are changing the habits of a lifetime as we learn to speak from the heart. Are we able to welcome our own and each other's stuttering, stumbling, and silences as signs that we are replacing automatic pilot with conscious speech? When we ask ourselves questions like the following, our words may indeed take more time to form:

- "What am I really reacting to here?"

- "What is the intention behind my opening my mouth now?"

- "What feelings are alive in me in this moment?"

- "What is the need behind my immediate desire here?"

- "Am I making a clear request of anyone?"

We might encourage a slower pace in our gatherings by, for example:

- Including moments of silence as a time for people to connect to themselves.

- Passing a talking stick (or other object) for some parts of the gathering. The person with the stick is offered the circle's gift of attentive silence without pressure to hurry. Generally, the stick is passed in one direction without interruption or comment from others. Individuals may choose to talk, or hold the stick in silence and pass it on without talking.

- Repeating, paraphrasing, or translating into NVC what one person has said before the next person speaks. This can be especially helpful when more than one person in the group is experiencing emotional intensity. To practice, the group might allot a certain amount of time during a meeting to interact in this way. This can also serve as an effective way to train our ability to listen.

- Taking two full breaths before speaking after the previous person has finished speaking.

◎ **3. What Might An Individual Do?**

As part of your intentional practice, it is as important for you to Remember Your Purpose and Take Time as it is for a group to do the same. Practice taking your time when you are responding to your family, friends, and co-workers.

C—Leading the Practice Circle

Each member has an opportunity for service and self-expression when offering to the circle his or her own unique way of leading the session. Because leadership is rotated, individuals may feel freer to take risks and explore their varying leadership styles. One leader's tendency towards rigidity and another's towards levity can combine to offer the group balance and diversity over time.

Leaders serve the circle in four ways:

1. They uphold the purpose of the circle by creating a space, remembering to slow down, incorporating opportunities to express appreciation, etc.

2. They oversee the group's practical and logistical needs.

3. They plan the structure (schedule of activities, etc.) and guide the group through the process.

4. They put extra effort into familiarizing themselves with the week's curriculum (or the contents of any materials to be covered) so they can be a resource for those who haven't familiarized themselves with it as well as the leader has.

The number of ways in which leaders can work or play with these four areas is infinite. Seasoned leaders will hopefully draw fully from their experiences so the circle may benefit from their facility, insights, and past mistakes. For those new to leading and facilitating, the following "Suggestions and Sample Format for Leading a Circle" can serve as a guideline from which to explore and experiment. Rooted in a consciousness of needs, we might remind ourselves that there is no "right way" to lead a circle, and no wrong way. There is only: my way (today, last month), your way (last week, last year), needs met, needs unmet . . .

Suggestions and Sample Format for Leading a Circle

The following section contains suggestions and a sample format for leading a circle that meets for two-and-one-half hours.

For the first meeting you lead, consider using the following suggestions, and on a separate piece of paper:

- make note of the suggested tasks as you complete them

- write down alternative ideas of how to proceed, while addressing the same objectives

- jot down what you plan to say in the circle at a particular step

- or organize your own plan.

Before the meeting

1. Read the chapter and complete the written assignment or whatever material the group has decided to cover.

2. Create a plan for the meeting—what's to happen, when, and how—or use the sample format as outlined below.

On the day of the meeting

1. Preparing the space
    Arrive 15 minutes early to arrange the seats in a circle so everyone will be able to see each other. If beverages are being made available, prepare cups, tea, etc., ahead of time. Arrange the centerpiece, wall charts, etc., if you choose to use these. A clock visible to all may be helpful.

2. Greetings
    Welcome each person as he or she arrives.

3. Connect with yourself
    When you are ready to begin, take 30 seconds to connect inwardly: "What do I feel and need right now?" Connect to the purpose behind what you are about to offer to the group. Be simply and fully present for one moment.

4. "Remembrance"
    Gather the group. Dedicate a moment to help us remember who we are and why we are here. Whether it's the change of seasons

or the bombings of overseas neighbors, focus on whatever inspires you yourself to feel connected to the web of life.

5. Opening the circle

Invite people to "check in" by sharing what is alive for them in this moment. Or, you might ask for a round of response to a question such as, "What kinds of NVC-related insights and experiences did you have this week?", or "Would you share something you would like to celebrate this week?" Indicate how much time you planned for the round; and then mention a general expectation of how much time you'd like each person to take. Go in one direction (clockwise or counterclockwise). Allow the group to focus attention on each person in turn. Either pass a talking object, or suggest a word, sound, or gesture that allows people to indicate they are complete before the next person begins. Remind participants to connect with their feelings and needs as they speak.

Example: "I'd like to open the circle with a round of check-ins. Let's take 20 minutes for this sharing—about three minutes for each of us. I'll start and then I'll pass this 'Talking Stick' clockwise. Let's practice staying connected to our feelings and needs as we speak. And remember, you have the option to talk or just enjoy the silence of holding the Talking Stick until you're ready to pass it on."

NOTE: After the round is complete, if you sense that someone who had shared vulnerably may still be carrying intense feelings, you might want to address them, acknowledge their words, empathize with their feelings and needs, or express your sincere reaction.

Before moving on, briefly state the schedule for the rest of the meeting.

6. Allow about 45 minutes for the first study or practice session. (This will likely begin about half an hour into the meeting.)

7. Mid-meeting, take a short break if desired.

8. Continue with a second study or practice session for another 45 minutes. (Use the Leader's Guide for each assignment to plan the study or practice sessions of the meeting.)

9. Feedback, appreciations, and closing (consider allowing 20-30 minutes). End the meeting with another "round." You might want a moment of silence to allow people to transition out of the Study or Practice Session. Invite them to connect with any feelings of gratitude that may be inside. Get in touch with any feelings of gratitude you might have for the opportunity of having served the circle in this way today.

    When you speak again, ask for feedback about the meeting. If you feel anxious when making this request, try expressing your feelings and needs and any request that might address those needs.

    Formally close the circle (whether with words, music, silence, poetry, a joining of hands, or other means of your choosing).

10. Post-meeting details

    a. Confirm who will be the leader for the next meeting and finalize other practical details.

    b. Ask everyone to take 5 minutes to fill out an "Individual Feedback Form" (See Appendix 5) while the meeting's experience is still fresh in their minds.

    c. Clean up, pack up, farewells, departure.

After the meeting

Take time to ask yourself what you enjoyed and didn't enjoy about leading the circle, what worked and didn't work, and what you would want to do differently the next time. Read over the Individual Feedback Forms that group members wrote for you. Use the reverse side of your own Individual Feedback Form to reflect upon your experience.

If you sense yourself needing some empathy or understanding, you might approach a friend who listens to you well. If your pain is associated with someone's words or behavior that occurred in the circle, consider how you might protect trust in the circle while also meeting your needs for empathy and support.

If you feel joyous, elated, or proud of how you led the circle, find ways to acknowledge your growth and accomplishment. You might want to celebrate it at next week's Opening Circle.

D–"What We Value in a Practice Group Leader"

Thirty NVC practitioners in Seattle reflected together on the topic, "What do I want in a practice group leader?" Below is a summary of their discussion. If you will be leading a group, use this list to remind yourself of qualities that participants value. You may also use this list as a way to solicit feedback from participants on various aspects of your leadership after a particular session. Do not compare yourself to the leaders being described in the italicized quotes below. They don't exist.

- **We value leaders who keep our group on task.**
  "She maintains the focus and is able to track interruptions and bring us back to the point. She starts the meeting at the agreed-on time and keeps track of time."

- **We value leaders who balance task orientation with an attention to process and who provide a clear structure, but are also able to let it go when that's called for.**
  "He covers the agenda without sacrificing the quality of the moment. He stays present and grounded, and sets a tone that fosters a positive atmosphere." "She is flexible with the process and the structure so as to meet everyone's needs."

- **We value leaders who "lead as servant to the group."**
  "He is eager to learn from us what we need and is responsive to feedback. The needs of the group is what is important to him."

- **We value leaders who pay attention to group dynamics.**
  "She is observant of everyone in the group and of interactions among members. She helps facilitate the process and encourages the group process without taking over or 'owning' the group. She knows how to help the group move forward or to stand still."

- **We value leaders who are aware of safety needs in the group and who create a space that emphasizes inclusiveness.**
  "He encourages everyone to participate and makes sure each person has the opportunity to speak and be heard. He maintains a balance so the group is not dominated by a few members." "She maintains a safe emotional environment and draws out the full

participation of those present so that they feel empowered to express themselves and be who they are."

- **We value leaders who embody compassion.**
  "He is open, empathic, and patient. He listens carefully without being judgmental."

- **We value leaders who are playful and have fun leading.**
  "She has a sense of humor and is lighthearted."

- **We value leaders who show humility, a willingness to acknowledge their own limitations, and the courage to take risks.**
  "He is vulnerable, recognizes his own limits and fears, and is able to ask for help. He is courageous in acknowledging what he doesn't know. He is willing to move out of the comfort zone into uncomfortable places."

- **We value leaders who come prepared and who keep their commitments.**
  "He plans for the meetings and is well-organized and takes seriously his commitment as a leader."

- **We value leaders who bring us back to expressing ourselves in NVC.**
  "She keeps within the process and helps us hear each other's feelings and needs clearly, especially when friction arises."

- **Other qualities we value in a practice group leader:**
  Clarity, Authenticity, Honesty, Creativity.

E—Making Rules

Agreeing on a set of rules for your practice circle can save time and be a source of reassurance that everyone is "on the same page." If you intend to post rules for your NVC practice group or organization, try the following NVC exercise:

1. Rules are strategies to meet needs—explore and express the need(s) behind the rule.

2. Ask yourselves, "Is this rule a request or a demand?" (Does anyone notice any "should, ought to, supposed to" thinking around it?)

Especially for a group that meets regularly, more satisfaction might be gained through ongoing dialogues regarding feelings, needs, and current requests than through rules—especially if the rules did not evolve out of group discussion of needs. Rules sometimes have the tendency to incline us towards judgment and blame when we encounter someone who has chosen to "break the rule." And thus, when someone does "break a rule"—for example, by missing meetings—on top of whatever we might be feeling towards that person's absence, we also experience an additional layer of pain regarding group rules not being respected.

If we have a need around which we are particularly anxious, e.g., confidentiality, rather than counting on everyone agreeing to a "confidentiality rule," we could try to articulate it: "I am worried about being understood or seen in ways other than I want to be. When I share something about my life in this circle, I get scared sometimes that one of you might tell someone else what I said and they'll get an impression of me I don't want them to have. I'd like to hear from the rest of you—do you have such fears too?"

We might request time to explore specific situations that trigger fears such as talking about other people in their absence. What needs are we meeting and what other ways could we meet those needs? How can we cultivate deeper awareness of intention when speaking about others? How can we support each other in living our intentions when talking about others? How can we check in on people's sense of comfort around this issue as the circle progresses?

It is possible that rules, by their identification with specific strategies, might actually hinder the cultivation of the transformative heart space where miracles take place—where joyously we let go of what a minute ago we thought we "had to have" out of the profoundly transformed realization that there is a superabundance of strategies for all needs to be met.

Of course, rules and laws do play a prominent role in our society. As NVC users, we can translate each one we come across so as to hear the need behind it as clearly as possible. More importantly, we try to stay connected to the need behind our own choice to either behave in accordance with the rule or not. In an NVC community, we know how much we will pay if anyone amongst us hears the group rules as demands, and then—woe—chooses to "follow the rules."

F—Inviting Feedback

Clear and accurate knowledge of how our words and actions affect others is a major resource for personal growth and the ability to communicate effectively. NVC stresses taking responsibility for one's own feelings as well as actions. Thus we are clear that our words and actions cannot "make" others feel nor do anything, and that other people's feelings derive from their own met or unmet needs.

However, we are also aware that all of us have tremendous power to contribute to the well-being (or lack of well-being) of others. If we take joy in contributing to life (our own well-being as well as that of others), we value feedback that shows us whether our intention to contribute has been realized. A bloated feeling in the stomach may be feedback from eating a 10-course banquet. Smiles from the delivery people may be feedback from my holding open the door for them. Several toots from the car behind me may be feedback on how I am backing up out of my parking space.

Most of us welcome feedback that confirms that our actions are indeed contributing to life. We may be less eager, however, to access feedback of the "negative" kind if we choose to hear it as judgment, condemnation, or demand. However, a bloated stomach is not a judgment of the banquet, a condemnation of my choice to gorge myself, or a demand never to indulge again. If we remember we always have power of choice and that the source of feedback can never "make" us behave differently, we might be able to appreciate feedback simply as precious information that helps us make more effective decisions. It is helpful to remember that choosing to hear another for the purpose of understanding their position in no way implies alignment or agreement—only a willingness to connect with them in order to accurately understand what is alive in them in this moment.

In an NVC practice group we all share a commitment to deepen our capacity for compassion, connection, and communication. Belonging to an NVC practice group can be a gold mine for those who value feedback. Be sure to reserve time at the end of each group session for reflection, mutual appreciation, and feedback. Appendices 5 and 6 are individual and group feedback forms used by some practice groups.

G—Conflicts in the Group

Part of the richness and challenge of working and learning in a group is having our buttons pushed. Most of us will probably experience some tension and conflict in a group that meets over time. Our most important NVC-based task is to move into awareness of what we feel and need when we sense conflict. With this awareness we can make a conscious choice as to how to address our needs in a way most likely to bring us fulfillment.

Whereas we might unconsciously suppress or ignore tension we feel around people in other groups, it sometimes happens in an NVC practice group that we react to unpleasant situations by exposing our fellow group members to every frustration, annoyance and anger they trigger in us with the assumption that this is "the NVC way." When we first experience the excitement of connecting with our own needs, we may forget that in the long run we can't meet our needs at the expense of others. Conflict is surely wonderful grist for the mill, but we can still exercise judgment regarding the timing, the size of the grist, and the power of the mill. A mature practice group may be able to embrace full-blown conflicts that would have overwhelmed its members a few months earlier. We also need to remember that if unresolved conflicts do lead to members leaving, or the group dissolving, that this itself is a crucial moment to practice NVC (see number 11 below).

The following situations involving conflict or dissatisfaction are common in NVC practice groups in some communities. The bold and quoted words come directly from participants. Commentaries follow in regular type. If you are experiencing any of the difficult situations mentioned below, use the words of the group member quoted to help get in touch with your own feelings and needs. The following list may also be used to engender role-play or real-time dialogue in your group.

1. Women, Men, and Other Differences

"Sometimes when a woman in the group is talking, I feel miffed because I would like to be enjoying the same level of understanding and catching the nuances that the women in the group all seem to be sharing with each other. I fear that I am losing some vital part of the conversation. I want to be participating fully while being seen and accepted for who I am and what I know."

This person expresses his need for inclusiveness—a value that is generally prominent when we participate in a group. He might want to ask himself what he is observing that leads him to think that the women are catching something he is missing. Did he notice glances between certain women? Was there laughter where he could detect nothing funny? By offering this kind of observation, he might help the women become aware of behaviors that may not even have been conscious, but more importantly, he can express his feelings and needs and ask for empathy from the women. If he were able to obtain the reassurance that the women understand and care that he feels lonely and miffed and needs to be included, he may well experience connection and acceptance even if he continues to be perplexed by the humor of certain moments.

In a group where we perceive ourselves as "minority," we can (after expressing our needs) make specific requests for behaviors that we think would support our needs for inclusiveness or respect. For example: "Would you be willing to use words other than 'sexist' to describe what you are reacting to?" In a diverse group, our need for inclusiveness can still be met even if we never "get" what all the others who share a common background might be "getting." What will make a difference is whether we achieve the trust and reassurance that a significant number of those present (and that could be just one person) hear our pain and sincerely care about our needs to be fully included, accepted, and respected.

2. Practicing vs. Talking About a Situation

"I get frustrated each time we agree to do role-plays and then end up talking <u>about</u> the situations people bring up. I am confused as to why this happens."

After acknowledging this concern openly to the group, we may want to review Section K, *Suggestions for Structuring a Role-play*, to make sure that everyone in the group is clear about the purpose and process of role-playing. If the group continues to find itself talking about the situation rather than practicing, it could be that the central person (whose life situation it is) is in a great deal of pain and needs empathy before being able to carry on a role-play. In this case, we can either move into an "unrealistic scenario" whereby the central person receives empathy from the other party (See Section K, *Suggestions for Structuring a Role-play*, #2), or stop the role-play and switch to an empathy session (See Section J, *Suggestions for Structuring an Empathy Session.*)

Here's an example of what one might say to address the situation:

"I'm concerned that we might be talking about this scenario rather than practicing it. I wonder if it would be helpful, (name of central player), if you could be more fully heard and understood about the situation before we engage in this role-play? How would you feel about just relaxing into an empathy session and having us focus on listening and reflecting back your present feelings and needs around this past situation?"

3. Structure: Tight or Loose?

These things occur:

- people arrive late . . .

- then they socialize with each other . . .

- the facilitator starts the check-in 20 minutes after agreed-upon time . . .

- people give their thoughts and opinions on various subjects more-or-less NVC-related—most often 'less' . . .

- they talk at length (more words than I'd like to hear) and about stuff I have no interest in . . .

- the check-in takes 45 minutes . . .

- the facilitator seems to go with the flow (It seems we just go with whoever wants to talk about whatever) . . .

"I get frustrated because I want to be devoting my time here to practicing NVC."

This speaker values group time and wants it mindfully used in service of the original purpose for which the group was formed: "practicing NVC." Before expressing himself to the group, he might want to clarify for himself what he means by "practicing NVC," and be open to other members' definitions. After he communicates his frustration and need, and receives empathy and understanding, he may want to hear how others have experienced the triggers he mentioned. He may discover, for example, that someone who has been arriving late was also frustrated with the tardiness, or why someone would prize the 45-minute check-in more than any other activity of the meeting. It may be helpful to engage in a Reflective Round (See Section I, *Forms of Group Interaction*) repeatedly until all needs and feelings regarding this subject have been heard, and only then begin to explore solutions. If agreements are made at the end of the discussion, end with another Reflective Round, in which all members express their feelings about the agreements and what needs of theirs are met by agreeing to them.

4. "Real-Time" Interactions vs. Planned Practice, Getting Angry before getting to the Anger Chapter, and More on Structure

As mentioned in the section *Creating a Practice Group*, while all members may share basic reasons for coming together, we may place different values on different aspects of our NVC group experience. Some people value "real-time" interactions, whereas others want to focus on practice through role-plays, exercises, assignments, etc. Many of us, like the person below, want to balance and include both:

"I feel anxious and torn when I hear people expressing pain, sometimes during check-in, because I want us to take time to empathize and I also want us to complete the check-ins to get to the rest of our planned practice session."

It is helpful for a group to openly acknowledge this as an ongoing tension—and one that can call forth different responses as the group grows in its mastery of NVC. We refer jokingly to the problem of "getting angry before getting to *Expressing Anger Fully*" when using this chapter-a-week curriculum. Until the NVC process (2 parts and 4 components) has been covered, it may be helpful for a group to limit interactions about real-time situations to a specific part of the session, e.g. check-ins. This ensures that the group spends more time practicing and learning NVC than discussing opinions, past experiences, theories, and personal situations. Once all the basics of the process have been covered (by the eighth week), the group will be able to incorporate Empathy Sessions. As individuals achieve greater NVC fluency, more and more of the session may consist of unstructured real-time NVC interactions.

In any group we commonly find some members who want more structure and some who want less. It is helpful, if I want more structure, to be able to express often—and with specificity—how I appreciated the structured exercise that the group just completed. Likewise, if I appreciate less structure, I could make a conscious effort to specify ways in which I benefited from an opportunity to interact in real time.

5. Following Through on Group Agreements

"I get frustrated when we had agreed to incorporate a time for feedback at the end of every session, but only twice in these many meetings has the session's facilitator alerted us in time to do this. I want to be able to count on things happening as we all agreed."

If this person is clear that she values not only reliability, but also learning and connection—which she hopes to receive through regular feedback—she can address these distinct sets of needs separately with the group. As always, she will want first to be received and to know that her needs have been understood. Then other members might express how they have experienced the lack of feedback. Then separately, the lack of follow-through can be addressed in the same way. It is only after everyone's feelings and needs regarding each issue have been heard that the group would then launch into strategies and solutions.

6. When We Want Our Energy and Commitment to be Matched by Others

"When I see someone miss over three quarters of our meetings and arrive without having read the book or done the assignment, I feel frustrated because I would like to see more commitment and contribution on their part. I want to belong to a group where we are mutually supported by each other's commitment and efforts. (I am also confused and would like to understand why someone who participates so little still wants to be part of our circle.)"

It is easy for us to assume that someone's repeated absence and lack of preparation reflect a lack of interest without checking it out with the person. The lack of participation by other members may trigger discouragement, self-doubt, and frustration in us, especially if we ourselves are striving hard to live up to our commitment (because maybe not all our own needs are being met in the group). It would be useful to stop and find out from them whether their absence is related to needs of theirs not being met in the group (hence their lack of enthusiasm in participating) or to other circumstances. We might, for example, get an altogether different response such as:

"Even though I've been only making meetings once a month, this circle is a huge thing to me. The support and learning I get here are like an anchor for the rest of my crazy life. I am so exhausted when I get here after work and the long drive that I don't arrive very energetic, and I know this sounds crazy, but I can't tell you how much I appreciate just being able to soak up the peace and compassion I feel in this room. And about those assignments, I've been a little embarrassed to say this, but I'm not a book person. I mean, I don't really read much, and that's not how I learn—through books, that is. But I remember nearly everything I hear, so it helps me just listening to you guys do the exercises here. I can understand you really want to see everyone putting in, and I do want to do my share. I'd like to know what I could do to contribute even if I can't make it to every meeting until I get that job transfer."

Or, you may discover that the other people indeed have not been feeling enthusiastic about attending the circle, in which case we remind ourselves quickly, "It's not about us. It's about needs."—needs of theirs that are met by being elsewhere, or needs of theirs that haven't been met by their being here.

7. Members Who "Dominate"

"Just about every week I see the same two people getting more air time than others. On occasion I have heard them raise their voices and talk louder than someone else who was just beginning to speak. I feel disappointed because I want everyone to have equal opportunity to speak and be heard. I want to be learning from everyone."

Many of us experience situations where certain people speak much more than we enjoy hearing. In our frustration and helplessness, unable to meet our needs for mutuality or connection, we may end up labeling the other person as "domineering," "insensitive," "exhausting," etc. In the chapter on *The Power of Empathy* in the book, there is a section that demonstrates how we might interrupt speakers rather than pretend to be listening to them.

In a practice group we may be uncomfortable with one person taking substantially more airtime even if we enjoy what she is saying, because we so value balanced participation. Since people who are perceived by others as "talking too much" aren't necessarily aware when their behavior falls into that category, they may appreciate some form of explicit feedback: raising a hand, for example, when we begin to feel uncomfortable and want the floor to be passed on. We might also consider structuring in more balance through the use of the Round, or a Talking Object (see Part III, Section I, *Forms of Group Interaction*), or we might even experiment with the game of talking-tokens, in which we all start off with an equal number of tokens and release one every time we take the floor.

8. "Doing NVC" as an Obstacle to Connection

"At times when I see people 'doing NVC' by parroting the process, I feel annoyed because my need is for authentic connection rather than correctness."

When we perceive ourselves being addressed through NVC formulas rather than through a living application of NVC concepts, it might be helpful to remember to stay connected to the concepts as they live within us. Remember once again that any form of anger like irritation or annoyance is likely to have its origin in "should thinking." While there is nothing "wrong" about thinking that way, we are much more likely to experience the authentic connection we hope for when we are able to translate such thinking into feelings and needs.

We are more likely to stay stuck in annoyance and conflict when we believe our feelings are caused by the actions of another like, "I feel annoyed because you are parroting the process." It benefits us to examine the feeling of annoyance to see if it is grounded in some thinking of how "authentic connection 'should' sound." Take a moment to re-center—a slow deep breath, etc. By spending a moment to get clearer about what is going on in you at a deeper level, you will be more open to hearing what is going on in the other person in relation to authentic connection. It may well be that the speaker also values authentic connection, and is relying on the process as the best means to establish connection.

If you are in some pain from seeing yourself being given "formulaic empathy," you might acknowledge it in this way: "I hear the conscious effort you are making to empathize with my position. I realize I'm experiencing difficulty in staying present and want what to me is a deeper sense of genuine connection between us. Would you be willing to work with me on that by expressing what you just said in a different way? What I really need to hear right now is, 'xxxxx?'" Or, you might make a clear and do-able request for honesty—for the other person to reveal what is going on in her in that moment. Take your time. Remember the energy from which you want to come, and your desire for her to respond to you only from her heart—willingly and without fear of consequences.

Oftentimes in moments of uncertainty, those who practice NVC refer to the steps of the process as a literal road map to point them step by step to the place of the heart. When we are willing to hear and see another person's intention rather than focus on their "stiff attempts to practice NVC," we may come to recognize how both our hearts share the same intention and desire for connection.

9. "Nice Yet Boring" Meetings

"I feel disappointed with the often 'nice yet boring' quality to our meetings. It doesn't meet my need for authentic connection."

Oftentimes it only takes one person to introduce something "real" in the circle for the group culture to deepen in intimacy and authenticity. If we are willing to be that person, we might first consider expressing our need, and then requesting feedback as to whether, when, or how other members would be willing to receive something we'd like to risk sharing.

Alternatively, we might initiate a dialogue on the subject, "Thinking about our meetings over the last four months, I sometimes feel disappointed that we don't seem to have touched any issues that generate strong feelings for us. I would like more depth and authenticity in our connection. May I hear from each of you how you have experienced this aspect of our gatherings?" Explore what fears might be preventing members from sharing more openly, and especially the needs behind the fears. Take time to empathize with each person before trying to decide how the group might change in a way that addresses the need for authenticity, as well as the other needs expressed.

10. A Lone Dissenter

"One person is unwilling to go with what the rest of us want, and says she will only practice in a particular way. I feel worried because I want cooperation and more consideration for what large numbers of people in the group want. And then, when I see how much of the group time and energy has been spent dealing with what this person wants, I start to feel resentful because I want to be spending time on the curriculum, and also to be enjoying a more fun, harmonious group atmosphere."

The pain in such a situation may be especially intense for one or more members of a practice group because we are constantly reminded of the importance of everyone's needs being met. Some of us are fearful of falling into behaviors we condemn, such as "tyranny of the majority," "stigmatizing," etc. We may thus feel depressed, hopeless, and frustrated—seeing ourselves stuck between either submitting to the will of a single person or asserting the power of the majority in ways we ourselves abhor.

Here we need to take a big breath, let it out, and recall the difference between needs and specific ways of meeting those needs. (Review the distinction between *need* and *request* in the NVC process. Requests consist of strategies that we hope might meet a need.) Can we let go of problem-solving for the time being, focus on nurturing empathy and connection in the group, and trust that when hearts connect, solutions will emerge? To truly connect will require us to share our frustrations—how hopeless we feel when we perceive no way out of our dilemma, how deeply we value inclusion and respect, how much we care about everyone's needs being met, etc.—and then invite the other person to express the feelings and needs triggered by her position as a "black sheep."

If we are able to offer each other empathy for the pain of this division in the group, we will be ready—out of that place of connection and compassion—to return and explore the original issue. We might agree to try some new strategies, or we might agree that, for all of us, the need for learning could best be met by the one person's joining a different learning situation. (See below, *When Someone Leaves.*) We can come to recognize that it is possible to disengage without disconnecting, to separate physically without putting each other out of our hearts.

11. When Someone Leaves or the Whole Group Dissolves

When a group loses a member or completely dissolves, it is common for everyone to feel pain, perceive failure, and exercise blame and self-blame. Thus it is a particularly crucial time to practice NVC. It would be helpful to remember that we can make conscious choices as to how we terminate a particular form of relationship. We can celebrate partings by openly acknowledging our differences, our pain and unmet needs, really devoting time to empathizing fully with each other, and also to expressing what we did appreciate during our time together. We can grieve our disappointments and still sincerely wish each other well as we move along different paths of engagement. Our work is to keep our hearts open to each other even while we choose different forms to meet our respective needs for learning, community, etc.

12. Mixed-Level Participants

Practice groups that include both newcomers to NVC and more seasoned practitioners may find it helpful to recognize a tension characteristic of mixed-level groups. Seasoned practitioners have likely witnessed and been inspired by the beauty and power of NVC interactions. Their own experience may well have taught them the pitfalls of common social behaviors such as analyzing, complimenting, story-telling, sympathizing, diagnosing, etc. When they see the group engaging in such behaviors, they may feel worried and frustrated because they would like NVC to be learned and practiced in a way that reflects NVC principles and understanding. Then when they do make suggestions to the group, they may be additionally frustrated to find themselves unable to convey these in a way that is heard and appreciated by those who have not yet personally experienced the effects of NVC. In fact, they may notice their suggestions trigger insecurity and resentment in the group, especially in the circle-holder working hard to lead the particular session.

Mixed-level groups might benefit from inviting the most seasoned among them to lead the circle, at least through Assignment 8 (by which time all participants will have hopefully learned the basics of the NVC process). This provides an opportunity for the experienced practitioner(s) to apply their NVC skills and serve the group in ways that are most likely to be appreciated by others.

The following are two dialogues that address "NVC Old-timers" who find themselves in a practice group with newcomers to NVC. The first dialogue is between the Old-timer and a friend—another seasoned practitioner who is not part of the group. The second dialogue is between the same Old-timer and a participant in the practice group who is fairly new to NVC.

Old-timer: *I've been feeling kind of frustrated a bunch of times at my practice group . . .*

Friend: *Oh, is it someone in your group who is new to NVC?*

Old-timer: *Yeah. Two or three times now I've seen something happen and I say, "If we want to do it in NVC, here's how you'd say it . . ." And the response I get back is, "No, don't tell me. You* *can do it that way, but I want to do it this way."*

Friend: *So I can see you're feeling a bit frustrated because . . .*

Old-timer: *Right! I've been studying and practicing for two years and I've made lots of mistakes and have at least a little bit more understanding and insight than when I started, and I'd like to be able to share these . . . to offer what I've learned to a group where most everyone is new to NVC . . .*

Friend: *So are you sad that your need to contribute in that way isn't being met?*

Old-timer: *I am . . . I'm sad. Also, I'm kind of angry.*

Friend: *Angry? Like when you hear how they respond to your trying to help?*

Old-timer: *Yes, I'm noticing I'm feeling somewhat angry . . . guess that means I must have some old "should" thinking going on in my head.*

Friend: *How about ferreting out those "should-thoughts?"*

Old-timer: *Oh yes, the "should-thinking" . . . Let's see. I guess I'm thinking, "They should listen to me. They should believe me, they should be able to see my intentions and know that what I am saying will help them."*

Friend: *Ummm, so to translate the "should-thinking" into needs . . .*

Old-timer: *(Silence. Then:) Yeah, I need to contribute, maybe to be trusted, and understood better. (Long silence)*

Friend: *Do you still feel angry?*

Old-timer: *Uhn-uh. No. I feel . . . I guess hurt.*

Friend: *Do you feel hurt because you want your intentions to be seen and appreciated? And what you offer to be received?*

Old-timer: *That's right. I want to be received, to be trusted and appreciated . . . (Silence as Old-timer stays present to feelings inside.)*

Friend: *I wonder if you also feel some discouragement because you want to be able to communicate your intentions in a way that is better understood?*

Old-timer: *Yeah, I feel disappointed with myself. I want to be more effective, more competent in applying this language of NVC. I want some reassurance that after two years I can communicate my intentions so I'm understood.*

Friend: *Well, maybe you're doing it right now. Am I getting what you want to communicate?*

Old-timer: *Yes, yes, you got it.*

Friend: *Then maybe you can do the same with the new folks. I see one of them from your practice group coming right now.*

Old-timer: *Yikes!*

Friend: *Yikes? I wonder if that translates in classical NVC into: "I feel scared; I would like more confidence than I have, and my request to myself is to go ahead and try it."*

Old-timer: *Uh . . . yes. Well, here goes . . .*

Dialogue between Old-timer and the Newcomer:

Old-timer: *Oh, hi. I've been meaning to talk to you. At the practice group a couple of times now, when I've suggested, "In order to say it in NVC, why don't you . . ." I heard you answer back something like, "No, I don't want to do it that way," or "I don't know that what you are saying is true . . ."*

Newcomer: *Yeah, it's real annoying when you tell us what to do! Like you're the only one who knows how to do it right. Okay, so you've been studying for two years, but that doesn't mean the rest of us don't know anything. I mean, a lot of us have been practicing compassion and communication, and . . . sure, yeah, you might know some things but I know other stuff.*

Old-timer: *So, am I hearing that you feel frustrated because you would like to be addressed differently—in a way that shows recognition for what you have learned, for what you know and for the efforts you are making?*

Newcomer: *That's right. I'm trying to do the best I can, and I feel annoyed when someone interrupts and tells me I gotta do it this way, or I gotta do it that way. I mean, I want to learn NVC, of course, that's why I'm in a practice group. I want to benefit from the more experienced people, but I don't want to be told I'm wrong, you're right, now do this, now do that!*

Old-timer: *So you want to be offered choices, to hear there might be another way to do something, and to be given the opportunity to choose. Perhaps you also want respect for the choices you make? I mean, rather than being told, "Here is the right way," so do it!*

Newcomer: *Absolutely! Thank you, thank you! I see now that I have been hearing a demand from you. Sort of like, this is the right way, and if I don't do it your way, I'm stupid, stubborn, resistant, and in addition, dismissive and disrespectful towards you.*

Old-timer: *Wow! So are you really needing to trust that I am offering in a way that has no strings attached . . . an offer that is respectful of your choice to either use or not use my coaching, based on your learning style or particular learning needs for that moment?*

Newcomer: *That's exactly it. If I could trust that that's the spirit in which you are offering help, then I would probably be a lot more receptive to your suggestions . . . and probably even really appreciate some of them!*

Old-timer: *Mmmm. Yeah, I'd really enjoy that. In fact, that's what I started to talk to you about.*

Newcomer: *Right. I bet you were feeling upset because you really enjoy contributing and want to do it in a way that is appreciated. Would you be willing to let a Newcomer offer you some NVC empathy?"*

Old-timer: *I'd love it! . . . and . . . uh . . . would you be willing . . . ahem . . . to let me coach you on doing it?*

H—Embracing Conflict: Reminders

1. Slow down. Slow down again.

2. Ground yourself in PRESENT moment feelings and needs.

For example, two seconds ago as you were listening to someone talk, you might have felt exasperation. This moment, opening your mouth, you feel scared . . .

3. Focus on empathy and connection.

4. Ask for help.

For example, "Would you be willing to help me formulate my observations?"

5. Continue to empathize until everyone affirms that their feelings and needs have been understood.

6. ONLY then explore solutions.

"How do we see things happening differently in the future? Will there be changes in behavior on my or someone else's part?"

7. Celebrate our peacemaking

Acknowledge: our intention, courage, patience, perseverance, compassion, plain hard work, etc. Remind ourselves why we do this work and what is happening in the world in this moment.

I—Forms of Group Interaction

With an increase of participants in a dialogue, the potential for disconnection among them may also increase. In a leaderful NVC group the only guideline for a free-flowing discussion is for each person to remain aware of their own needs and values—free from moral judgments—and to take responsibility for fulfilling those needs. Of course these needs may include offering, as well as receiving, empathy for the sake of understanding, clarity, and connection.

Appendix 7 is a chart of the NVC process that may be used to track our interactions in relation to the two parts and four components of NVC. The following description of various forms of group interaction is offered for those groups that wish to experiment with structure.

1. Round

The Round creates a space for each person in turn to receive the attention of the group. Going around in one direction, speakers take turns and indicate when they are complete. There is no direct response to the speaker, although whoever has the floor may of course address anything that had been said earlier. When a speaker is complete, she or he gives a signal to pass on the turn. Anyone may pass without speaking or, on occasion, choose to receive the group's silent empathy before passing on their turn.

When starting a Round, the group might consider whether to specify:

   a. How much time to devote overall.

   b. The time allowance for each individual (and how and from whom time reminders are to be given).

   c. Subject matter, e.g. "Something meaningful in my life today," "My vision for this organization," "An NVC experience or insight," "Challenges I have as a teacher," etc.

   d. A word or gesture that a speaker uses to indicate completion.

   e. Whether to go around once, or to continue until everyone passes and wishes to say nothing more.

2. Reflective Round

In this variation of the Round, before taking his or her own turn, the person who comes after a speaker reflects back to the speaker's satisfaction what the speaker has just said. Speakers might clarify and repeat something if they are not satisfied that they have been fully understood. However, the purpose would be to clarify, not add to what they have already said. The Reflective Round is useful in slowing down the group process and supporting each person's need to be fully heard.

3. Talking Object

An object symbolic of group intentions is placed in the center of the circle. Anyone wishing to speak picks up the item to "claim the floor." The speaker may make requests of anyone in the group in order to address her needs. She continues to hold the item while others are responding to her request. Holding the item reminds the group and whoever is speaking that it is still her requests that are being addressed on the floor. When she has finished, she returns the item to the center and waits until others have had a turn before picking it up again.

4. Traffic Director or Facilitator

One person or a succession of persons is chosen by the group to direct group traffic or facilitate the meeting by doing some or all of the following:

a. Determine whose turn it is to speak.

b. Reflect back in NVC what the speaker said, or request specific individuals to translate what was said (to support the group's ability to hear each other's feelings, needs, and clear requests).

c. Guide the flow of discussion, interject and ask for specific responses from specific individuals.

d. Articulate main points, decisions, and direction to bring coherence and cohesiveness into discussion.

5. Free Flow with Reflection

There is no "turn setting" in a free-flow interaction—we trust that each person is willing and able to address his or her own needs as they arise. As in the Reflective Round, however, before speaking, each person first reflects back to the satisfaction of the previous speaker what the previous speaker just said. This process encourages a group to slow down, listen carefully, and receive each speaker before moving on.

Speakers who are not satisfied with the reflection they receive may clarify themselves. Their intention, however, is to clarify rather than expand upon their original statements. The process bogs down if the speaker and reflector engage in a back-and-forth dialogue. If, after a couple of tries, the speaker is still dissatisfied with the reflection, the reflector might request another member of the group to carry on. When the speaker is finally satisfied, the floor returns to the original person who had wanted to speak next.

NOTE: MAKING CLEAR REQUESTS IN A GROUP.

No matter what form a group interaction takes, group process is greatly enhanced when speakers are aware of their intentions and are able to make clear and present requests each time they address the group. NVC offers the following suggestions to help a speaker specify what she would like from the group:

a. Clarify who you want to respond by naming a specific person or persons.

   Example: *I would like Jeanine and Harold to tell me . . .*

   Example: *I would like anyone who would care to tell me . . .*

   Example: *I would like two (3, 4, etc.) of you to tell me . . .*

b. Clarify the action you are requesting.

   Example: *I would like Jeanine and Harold to tell me (specify input wanted from them) . . .*

   Example: *I would like (specify people you are wanting to respond) everyone present to (specify action) raise your hand if you* (specify what you want the action to signify) *agree to end our meeting at 5:00 p.m.*

When you are asking several people to take turns responding to you, it may be helpful to clarify the order in which you want them to respond:

Example: *I would like to hear from each of you your reasons for being here. I would like to start on my left and go around the group clockwise.*

c. Signal when your requests have been fulfilled to your satisfaction and you are ready for someone else to take the floor.

Example: *I am finished.*

J—Suggestions for Structuring an Empathy Session

An "Empathy Session" allows a member to receive genuine, in-the-moment empathy for a meaningful live situation, while providing clear roles for others within a structured NVC practice activity. Consider the following suggestions while developing your own structure and guidelines. You may notice that as your circle matures over months and years, earlier established (and more rigid) guidelines might increasingly give way to a spontaneous flow.

Prior to beginning, consider taking a moment to reconnect with the heart: slow down, and re-presence yourself. One way is to stop, breathe, and consciously reflect on the energy we wish to cultivate. A guided imagery recited by a group member, a song, or a moment of silence can remind us of our intention to stay with empathy, compassion, clarity, or requests that demonstrate respect for *all* concerned, including oneself. It can help set the tone and ground us in heart energy as we focus on "preparing to do something."

1. Decide on the length of the Empathy Session. You might try 15 minutes of empathy with 5 minutes for processing afterwards.

2. Decide how many Empathy Sessions you would like to include in today's meeting. If there are more members than sessions, decide when you will have further Empathy Sessions so that everyone will have an opportunity to receive empathy.

3. Decide who will be the Speaker. Often a member who is experiencing urgency around a painful situation will volunteer. Or, it could be someone who has not had a chance to be Speaker yet.

4. The Speaker is urged to speak about a situation that does not involve anyone in the circle, and is minimally likely to trigger pain in anyone present.

5. Reassure the Speaker that she or he will have the full allotted time, and that when Listeners interrupt, the intention will not be to "take the floor away" from the Speaker, but to reflect back and make sure that the Speaker's words have been accurately received.

6. The Speaker is urged to pause often to give Listeners an opportunity to reflect back. Marshall Rosenberg suggests a 40-word limit! While most of us, especially when we are in pain, may go beyond 40 words, it is useful to remember to offer words in smaller chunks if we want our Listeners to fully hear everything we are saying.

7. Speakers may choose to practice NVC or they may choose to express themselves in habitual ways, entrusting the work of NVC translation to the Listeners. The primary objective of Empathy Sessions is to provide practice in deep listening and verbalizing empathy. For this practice, do not encourage Speakers to struggle to "speak NVC." The role of Listeners in this activity is to listen, not to coach the Speaker in expressing herself in NVC.

8. Decide on who will take the role of Timekeeper.

9. Decide whether you would like one person to be the active Listener (who reflects back) or to have the whole group participate, taking turns verbalizing empathy to the Speaker. Relying

on the whole group means everyone is an equally active participant; it may also offer the Speaker a wider opportunity to be fully understood. However, Speakers may experience distraction, because it is sometimes difficult to sustain fluid transitions when different people take turns verbalizing empathy. A third alternative is for the Primary Listener to exercise the choice—each time when the Speaker pauses—to either empathize or to pass it onto the group. This little bit of added direction on the part of a Primary Listener is often enough to make the process sufficiently smooth to include the active participation of more people.

NOTE: If more than one person is offering empathy to the Speaker, a competitive tone can sometimes enter the circle, with each Listener trying to "get it right" (accurately guessing the Speaker's feelings and needs). Then we need to remind ourselves that empathy is not about accuracy, but about the quality of our attention.

---

10. Timekeeper: begin the session with a 30-second silence to allow the Speaker to become focused. Listeners, use this moment to connect with your intention to be fully present, to listen with your whole being.

11. Listeners attend fully to the Speakers and their words, while sensing the feelings and needs beneath the words. Your objective is to be totally present, not to "figure out" what the Speaker is feeling and needing nor to "get it right."

12. When the Speaker pauses, the Listener will reflect back verbal empathy. Listeners may also interrupt the Speaker in order to reflect back—especially if they are getting more information than they can take in at one time, or if they are not clear about what was just said.

13. Listeners, try to empathize verbally, translating what the Speaker is saying into observations, feelings, needs, and requests* (see note, page 49). We reflect back in an asking (rather than telling) way: Is this what you were observing, feeling, and needing?

(Speakers are always their own authority on what they saw [heard, etc.], feel, or need.)

Example:

Speaker: *My boss keeps putting me down . . .*

Listener: *So you've heard your boss say things about you, or to you, that haven't been meeting your need for respect?*

Speaker: *Yeah, he says things to me, like yesterday he said . . . I don't even know as much as the fellow who came in from the temp agency . . .*

Listener: *Hearing him say that . . . do you feel upset and want some acknowledgment . . . some appreciation for what you've done at the office?*

Speaker: *(continues on)*

14. Listeners: Help Speakers return to the present moment even though they are describing a past situation.

Example:

Speaker: *I am really upset at my boss and the other department heads for pulling this one on us. It's just like when I was a kid, I remember my father would spring these surprise moves on us. Once he told us two days before the moving van arrived, that we were relocating to Canada! I mean, two days! And then I found out he had signed the job contract half a year earlier!*

Listener: *So when you remember how your father waited to tell you about the relocation, do you still feel angry and hurt because you want your needs to be taken into consideration around decisions that affect your life?*

NOTE: Listener, you are not focusing on the current interaction between yourself and the Speaker. The "request" that you are reflecting back is not what the Speaker is wanting from you right now, but what the Speaker was wanting in the situation being described. During Empathy

Sessions, we avoid focusing on problem solving unless (or until) the Speaker makes such a request in the closing round.

For example, if the Speaker says, "She's a hypocrite!" the listener might:

Reflect back need: *You value integrity? You'd like to see people walking their talk?*

Reflect back request: *You see her campaigning for animal rights, and* (request) *so you want her to use cruelty-free cosmetics herself?*

---

15. Timekeeper: Let the circle know when the time is nearly up (e.g. "We have three minutes left."). Make another announcement when the time is up. If the Speaker is in the midst of expressing intense feelings, or if you sense a lot of unfinished pain in the circle, you (the Timekeeper) might ask if the Speaker would like to receive a minute of silent empathy before the group moves into closing the Empathy Session. Everyone then remains fully present with the Speaker (who no longer speaks), while continuing to sense the feelings and needs behind the Speaker's silence. The Timekeeper indicates the end of one minute.

16. Finish the Empathy Session with two rounds. When scheduling an Empathy Session, plan an additional five minutes to cover the two closing rounds.

    a. The Speaker begins the first round by making any request he or she might have of the group. Oftentimes when we have allowed ourselves to be vulnerable, we may want to know afterwards how others feel about what we shared. Or the Speaker may make a request for advice, opinions, information, etc., from the group to address the issue that was expressed. Go around in a circle so that each person has an opportunity to respond to the Speaker's request.

    b. Close with a second round where each person expresses insights, feelings, etc., regarding the process just completed or about their own role in the Empathy Session. This may also be an opportunity for offering appreciation to each other for the learning and sharing that were received.

K—Suggestions for Structuring a Role-play

1. Participant A defines the situation by stating:

    a. Her own role: "I'm a temporary employee at a research lab."

    b. The role she wants Participant B to take: "You're my immediate supervisor."

    c. The time or place of dialogue, if relevant: "It's 6:00 p.m. Friday as I am ready to leave work." and then,

    d. Gives Participant B his first line (or first two lines): "So my boss says to me, 'Have you finished the report? I'd like to see it completed before we start the Monday morning meeting.'"

    Participant A: Offer further background information only if crucial for the other person to play his role. State the information briefly in one or two sentences. Avoid describing the situation, its history, or your experience of it. (Spend group time practicing a situation rather than explaining a situation.) If, during the role-play, Participant B is not playing to the role you want, simply cue him in: "No, you wouldn't say that. You'd probably say 'xyz.'"

2. Usually, Participant A practices speaking and listening empathically while Participant B speaks in a habitual manner. However, if Participant A experiences a lot of pain around the situation, she may find herself getting stuck in the role-play without being able to empathize with Participant B.

    In this case, it may be helpful to first enact an "unrealistic" scenario where Participant B, transformed into an NVC communicator, empathizes with Participant A. When the latter senses herself ready for the switch (and she may not during this role play), start over again, this time with Participant B playing the role realistically, using habitual speech.

    Another alternative is for Participant A to play the role of the non-NVC speaking supervisor, and hear how another person might play herself as someone fluent in NVC.

You may find it helpful to set a time limit for each role-play and to have a timekeeper. Be sure to allow opportunity at the end for both Participant A and Participant B to express what "worked," "didn't work," and what they learned. Observers of role-plays often have insights to offer as well.

PART IV
EXERCISES

*Assignments,
Leader's Guides,
and Sample Responses*

Assignments, Leader's Guides, and Sample Responses

Note to Individuals:

You can use all the following Reading Review and Individual Practice sections, as well as most of the activities in the Leader's Guides, on your own with little or no modification. Keep your notebook or computer handy to record your responses—feelings, needs, and ideas—as they arise. To assist you in completing Assignments and Activities, look for the symbol at the left and the notes to individuals that accompany it.

Individual learners motivated to invest more time and energy in learning this new language can create additional support for themselves. Using the four parts of the process, invite friends who are unfamiliar with NVC to assist you in staying in the land of observations, feelings, needs, and clear requests. Consider giving your friends the set of Quick Cards (see the list of Nonviolent Communication Materials at the end of this book), three colorful, laminated cards containing: the four steps of the NVC process, feelings when needs are—and are not—being met, and basic needs we all have. These at-a-glance tools will help them to interact with you in ways that support your learning. You might approach a friend, expressing yourself using the four components of the NVC process: *"When I practice NVC, I feel excited because I experience more fun* (intimacy, meaning, harmony) *in my relationships with my family* (friends, colleagues). *Please tell me, would you be interested in hearing how you can help me practice?"*

Another example for asking for this support from a friend is: *"When I think how relationships with my family are* (more fun, more meaningful, easier for all concerned, transformed before my eyes, etc.) *when I practice NVC, I feel excited because my need for harmony and predictability is met more often than before. I wonder if, after you hear what might be involved, you'd be willing to tell me if helping me practice sounds like something you'd like to do?"*

As you continue to practice with those who agree to help you learn the process, many will find value for themselves in speaking from the heart in this way. As that happens, review the sections of the workbook written to assist you in creating a structured practice group, and invite your friends to join you, using these suggestions in whatever ways feel comfortable for you.

Between now and then, continue to study the workbook as it addresses issues an individual may have that are similar to those a group might experience. Many of the suggestions addressing group practice throughout the workbook are equally applicable to an individual's practice.

As an individual using this workbook you may be tempted to look ahead to the Leader's Guides and Sample Responses before doing the assignments on your own. Doing the assignments on your own before reviewing the following sections will help you gain the maximum benefit from your efforts.

Exercises for the Chapter: Giving From the Heart

One—Individual Assignments

Reading Review

1. The author, Marshall B. Rosenberg, says that NVC evolved out of his exploration of two questions that had occupied him since childhood. These two questions are:

2. "Nonviolent Communication" is also known by the title, "_____," "NVC," or in some countries, "Giraffe Language." Some people have expressed discomfort with the word "nonviolent" in the title because they don't perceive themselves engaging in "violent" speech. How does Marshall explain the use of the word "nonviolent" in "Nonviolent Communication?" (*Please note: when used in this context, "nonviolent" is one word, without a hyphen.*)

3. What is the purpose of NVC?

4. How does it differ from the way we often communicate?

5. What is Marshall referring to when he writes that NVC is "more than a process or a language?"

6. Name the two parts of the NVC process.

7. Name the four components of the NVC process.

8. Mention some areas or ways in which NVC can be used in our lives and our society.

Individual Practice

Marshall Rosenberg tells the following story to illustrate the heart of Nonviolent Communication:

Waiting for a bus at the Greyhound Bus Terminal in San Francisco, I saw a sign on the wall: "Teenagers: Do Not Talk to Strangers." The evident purpose of the sign was to alert runaway teenagers to the dangers that await them in large cities: pimps, for example, are known to stalk lonely, frightened teenagers at terminals. With practiced warmth, they offer friendship, food, a place to stay, perhaps some drugs. Before long, they have trapped the teenagers into prostituting for them.

I felt sickened by this reminder of how human beings can be so predatory, but as I walked into the waiting area, my spirits lifted almost immediately. There I saw an elderly migrant farm worker with an orange on his lap. It was all that remained of his brown-bag lunch, which he had apparently just finished eating. Across the room, a toddler nestled in his mother's lap was staring at the man's orange. Noticing the child's gaze, the man immediately stood up and walked towards him. As he drew near, he looked at the boy's mother, and with a gesture, asked her permission to give the orange to the boy. The mother smiled. Just before reaching the child, however, the man stopped, cradled the orange in both hands, and kissed it. He then handed it to the child.

Sitting down next to the man, I told him that I was moved by what I had seen him do. He smiled, seeming pleased to have his act appreciated. "I was particularly touched by your kissing the orange before giving it to the boy," I added. He was silent for a few moments, his expression earnest, before he finally responded, "I have lived for 65 years, and if there is one thing I have learned, it is never to give unless I give from the heart."

Connecting with Our Intention

1. Find a place where you enjoy being and may be undisturbed for at least half an hour.

   a. Take some conscious breaths to quiet your mind and body.

b. Notice your environment: what do you see, hear, smell, feel in this place?

c. Before you turn your attention to the questions that are coming up, check to see how you feel and what your body is experiencing. Do you feel agitated, bored, tranquil, melancholic . . . ? Are you holding tension in your face, shoulders, back, left little toe . . . ?

2. Remember Marshall's story of the orange and see if you can recall an occasion in your own life that illustrates the joy of giving from the heart—or of receiving a gift that was given from the heart. *"I never feel more given to than when you take from me . . . When you give to me, I give you my receiving. When you take from me, I feel so given to."* (From Ruth Bebermeyer's song, "Given To.")

3. Ask yourself, "What draws me to practicing NVC? What is it that I deeply wish for in my life and in this world?" Just stay for a few moments with this desire, this need.

4. Do you remember a time in your childhood or more recent past when you have been aware of these needs or desires? What moments or parts of your current life reflect the presence of these needs?

NOTE: As you allow your mind to wander, recollect, ruminate, etc., stop occasionally to take a few conscious breaths and return to your body, staying connected with whatever physical sensations or feelings may arise before continuing with your contemplation.

---

5. Be aware when the intention arises in your mind to end this exercise (before you actually put away this workbook, get up, walk away, etc.) Once again, take a moment to pause and breathe. How do you feel in this moment? Are you aware of any fulfilled or unfulfilled needs? Allow a moment to notice your environment—what you are seeing, hearing, touching, smelling—before you depart.

During the course of this week, identify:

1. Occasions where you are giving from the heart. Remember, this doesn't have to be a "big deal." We are constantly "giving" of ourselves and our resources, whether it's a word of encouragement to a co-worker, holding the door open for someone, or telling a joke to the impatient child waiting in line at the supermarket. Describe how you feel when recalling the occasion.

2. An occasion where you are giving from some place other than the heart. Describe how you feel when recalling this event without judging or analyzing yourself or the event. What would you like to have happened on this occasion?

Write down how you responded to the above exercises, and any observations and learning you might have gained over the week.

NOTE: Most of us prefer to see ourselves as compassionate and generous people. We don't like to notice those moments when our hearts clamp shut or when we draw our hands back into our pockets. Yet it is by noticing over and over (without judging) those very moments when we have touched our limitations that we grow our compassion and generosity. Watch for those moments in yourself with a loving eye.

One—Leader's Guide

This first assignment gives us an opportunity to share something personally meaningful and to get to know each other. Take about an hour for Activity 1 (below), but allow enough time for all participants to fully share their stories of giving from the heart. If you run out of time, skip Activity 2.

Activity 1: Giving From the Heart

1. Ask each person to tell his or her story. (Take turns in a circle and let the group know how much time you have planned for this part. Encourage listeners to extend their full attention to speakers, recognizing that the telling of these stories may require courage and vulnerability on the part of speakers. At the end of each story, allow a few moments for the story to "sink in" and for the group to silently acknowledge the speaker before moving on to the next person. Discourage discussion or comments on peoples' stories.)

> Take a few minutes to think about your own story, making notes that speak to what is alive in you in this moment.

2. Invite individuals to share how they responded to the rest of the assignment. Some people might enjoy reading what they had written, while others might share their feelings about doing the exercises.

> Read what you've written in response to the exercise, and then express out loud your feelings about doing the exercise.

3. In ending this section, encourage the group to collectively summarize what was learned on the theme of Giving from the Heart. Before moving into Activity 2, check to see if there are

any other questions about Assignment One (including the Reading Review).

> ◎ Try identifying three things you learned on the theme of Giving from the Heart and record your responses in your notebook.

Activity 2: Seeing the Needs that Prevent Us from Giving from the Heart

Giving from the heart is one of the greatest joys we can experience, and is a foundational concept in Nonviolent Communication. But we all have needs that correspond to our giving that may sometimes interfere with true giving from the heart. We can learn to identify these needs.

1. Referring to any stories that were shared where the giving did not come from the heart, ask: "What need in that moment prevented you from doing so?" Mention: It is an assumption in Nonviolent Communication that using our power to contribute to other people's well-being is a source of deepest joy. If we don't find joy in it, then there are other needs present in us that we want to fulfill. Instead of labeling ourselves (or others) as "selfish," "uncaring," etc., we become aware that our choices of behavior are always in service of specific needs we are trying to meet. (This doesn't imply that our choices are always successful.)

> ◎ Recall a specific instance in which you gave something in a way that wasn't from the heart. Try to identify the true motivation behind the gift. Or remember a time you were asked for something and were unable to give it freely. Try to identify the needs that prevented you from giving what was asked. If any self-judgments come up during this exercise, simply notice you are entertaining those thoughts.

2. Invite those who have not done so to relate a moment when they did not give (or did not give from the heart) and to identify what need(s) of theirs prevented them from doing so. Use Appendix 3, Universal Needs List for reference, if necessary.

3. End this part by asking if anyone experiences a difference when their reluctance or refusal to give is understood as a choice to fulfill a need they have.

Think this through and record your response.

One—Sample Responses to Leader's Guide

Response for Activity 2: Seeing the Needs that Prevent Us from Giving from the Heart

When I was a child my father would say to me, "Get me a cup of tea." He never checked in with me to see what I might be doing at the moment, or whether I wanted to get him tea. I heard his words as a demand, and because I was fearful of the consequences of not complying, I would consistently drag my feet and grumpily bring him the cup of tea each time. Now he is dead, and as I write this, I feel so sad. I realize that he never received a cup of tea from me that was given from the heart. What prevented me from giving joyfully from the heart to him were my needs for respect and for autonomy.

It turned out, of course, that grumpy compliance was not a skillful strategy that successfully met my need for either autonomy or respect. I am sad now because I wish I had known how to better meet my needs for autonomy and respect, and then have been able to enjoy offering a cup of tea from the heart in a way that met my need for contribution.

Note: Responses will be highly individualized and based on personal experience.

 Review the sample response, noticing how it is similar to or different from your own.

Exercises for the Chapter: Communication that Blocks Compassion

Two—Individual Assignments

Reading Review

1. What is the meaning of "life-alienating communication?"

2. Name some forms of life-alienating communication, and give an example of each.

3. It's the author's belief that our analyses and judgments of other human beings are tragic expressions of _____.

4. Why does he use the word "tragic" to describe these ways of expressing ourselves?

5. What happens when people do what we want them to do out of fear, guilt, or shame?

6. When other people associate us in their minds with feelings of fear, guilt, or shame, what is likely to happen in the future?

7. What is the difference between value judgments and moralistic judgments?

8. Give examples of how words or phrases in the English language (or another language) obscure awareness of personal responsibility and choice.

9. What is a "demand" as defined by the author?

10. Marshall writes that his children taught him that he couldn't make them do anything. Explain what he means by that.

Individual Practice

1. Think of the forms of life-alienating communication as the "Four D's of Disconnection":

   a. Diagnosis, judgment, analysis, criticism, comparison

   b. Denial of responsibility

   c. Demand

   d. "Deserve"-oriented language

   Over the course of this week identify an instance of each category in your own speech, or if you wish, look back into your past. Choose an instance where you were communicating with someone else. Or, if you prefer, focus on your self-talk. Rather than describing the situation, write down the exact words you used.

2. Write down a dialogue (of about 6-8 lines) between two people that isn't going well. It could be a dialogue between you and another person in your own life. After you have completed writing down the lines, re-read them and determine if either person has communicated using one of the Four D's.

3. Choose one day this week as Four D-Alert Day. During this day, listen with heightened awareness to the way people around you are communicating. Whenever you hear a D, note and jot it down on paper. Do not forget to include what people are saying on TV, radio, and ads. You can include instances of both written and spoken words.

4. The author quotes French novelist George Bernanos: "The horrors which we have seen, and the still greater horrors we shall presently see, are not signs that rebels, insubordinate, untamable men are increasing in number throughout the world, but rather that there is a constant increase in the number of obedient,

docile men." (Note: He is likely implicating women too, even though he mentions only men.) Do you agree or disagree? Can you give examples?

5. Do you see ways that life-alienating communication benefits sociopolitical systems controlled by dictators, kings, and autocrats—or multinational corporations?

Two–Leader's Guide

Before you begin the activities, check to see whether anyone has strong interest in discussing the subjects raised in Individual Practice, questions #4 and #5 of the assignment. Skip Activity 3 altogether if there is only moderate interest. There may be more activities provided below than can be covered in your session without hurry. Try to allow plenty of time for Activity 1. Limit the time devoted to discussions so that more time is spent on practice than on discussion.

Activity 1: Written dialogue

If you have a white board or large piece of paper, take the dialogue you wrote for your assignment, Individual Practice, #2, and transcribe it so it can be read by the entire circle. (Do this before the meeting.) Assume the role of one person in the dialogue and ask someone else to take the other role and read the dialogue together out loud. Ask the group to identify forms of life-alienating communication in the dialogue.

 Review your sample dialogue and try to identify any of the four D's you see there.

After completing the above, go back and ask what unfulfilled needs the speakers might have been experiencing. (Refer to Appendix 3, *Universal Needs List* for this exercise.)

 Do this with your own dialogue.

Ask those who had written a dialogue to share their paper with a neighbor and to read the dialogue out loud together. The rest of the group (including the Leader) will take turns identifying the life-alienating forms of expression they hear. After you have done this for all the dialogues, go back and guess what unmet needs the various speakers might have had. Request to have the dialogues re-enacted with this in mind.

> ◉ Try asking a friend or partner to write a sample dialogue as in Individual Practice, #2. Review for unmet needs.

Activity 2: Four D-Alert Day

Ask how the week went, and what people noticed on Four D-Alert Day. Go around in a circle and ask everyone to either read what they brought or orally report their experiences. Allow a free flow of questions, perceptions and discussion on life-alienating communication—what people observe about their own habits and the language of our society. At the end have the group collectively summarize what they have learned.

Activity 3: Review of Questions #4 and #5

Take either or both Individual Practice questions #4 and #5 as the focal point of discussion. Unless there is passionate interest, limit this discussion to 15 minutes.

Activity 4: Identifying Life-alienating Messages

a. First ask people to name the arena(s) or communities in which they are active or with which they are identified. For example: education, nonprofits, parenting, meditation, corrections, NVC, etc.

b. Ask people if they notice specific messages that are prevalent in the arenas they mentioned. Allow three minutes of silence for reflection before group sharing. Examples for the arena of education:

- Teachers are supposed to give grades.

- Students who misbehave deserve to be punished.

- You have to attend school until you're 16.

- The American school system is abysmal.

Think this through and create a list for your own situation.

Two—Sample Responses to Leader's Guide

Responses for Activity 4: Identifying Life-alienating Messages

Examples of messages that are expressed in a way that is less likely to inspire compassionate cooperation in different areas:

Education

Demand language: "You have to attend school until you're 16."

Without demand: "We'd like you to attend school until you're 16 because we value a solid education."

Correctional Institutions

Deserve-oriented language: "People who hurt others deserve to be punished."

Without deserve-oriented language: "I'd like to see people who hurt others be given the opportunity to make amends for harm they caused because I value healing and restoration of trust."

NVC community

Diagnosis, judgment, criticism: "You're not speaking NVC."

Without diagnosis and criticism: "I'd like you to express your feelings and needs to me about this situation because I value honesty and connection."

Health

Denial of responsibility, diagnosis: "The doctor knows best."

Without denial of responsibility: "We ordered this test because we were hoping to get some definitive results."

Without diagnosis: "I would enjoy receiving your trust in my judgment of this matter."

Parenting

Demand language: "Adults must teach children how to behave in public."

Without demand: "I do so wish for adults to teach children to behave in ways that support the safety and quiet of public space."

Meditation

Denial of responsibility: "They made me sit there without moving for a whole hour."

Without denial of responsibility: "I chose to sit there without moving for a whole hour because I wanted to try out the teacher's instructions."

Exercises for the Chapter: Observing Without Evaluating

Three—Individual Assignments

Reading Review

1. In the lyrics quoted at the beginning of this chapter, the author pleads with listeners not to mix up two things. What are the two things he wants listeners to clearly separate when they are talking to him?

2. What is the reason for separating these two items (above)?

3. Explain the difference between "static language" and "process language."

4. Marshall prefers to avoid even positive or neutral labels of people, for example: "a responsible child," "a cook," "a pretty blond." Why?

5. What were some of the staff's evaluations of the school principal? What was a specific observation they made of the principal?

6. Do the words "always," "never," "ever," "whenever," etc. express observations or observations mixed with evaluation?

7. What is the first component of Nonviolent Communication?

Individual Practice

1. Write down three observations about yourself. Write three evaluations about yourself.

2. Give an example illustrating the difference between "static" and "process" language.

3. Refer to the table at the end of the Chapter that lists seven forms of

communication. Make up an example for each form, starting with an observation that is mixed with evaluation, followed by an observation free of evaluation.

4. Give an example in which the following words express an observation. Give another example in which they express an observation mixed with evaluation.

    a. "never"

    b. "always"

    c. "whenever"

    d. "constantly"

    e. "nobody"

5. The next time you are waiting in line, on a bus, or among a crowd of people, take five minutes to look at the people around you. What thoughts do you discover in your mind? If you have the opportunity, write down your thoughts, and examine them. Are they observations? Evaluations? What's the proportion of thoughts that are only observations to those that are mixed with evaluation?

Three—Leader's Guide

Explain that you have a series of exercises for the group, and that there may not be time to go over all pieces of the assignment they did over the week. Ask if there is anything that is especially important for anyone to cover today.

Activity 1: Observation or Evaluation?

Lead the Observation or Evaluation Exercise that is found in the book either at the end of the Chapter (Exercise 1) or at the end of the book (Practice 1). (Location depends on edition of book you're using.) Decide on your group's responses, and then check them with Marshall's.

(Note: If many people in your circle have previously done this on their own, use the following alternative exercise.)

Alternative Activity 1: Observation or Evaluation?

For the following statements, do you regard the speaker to be making an observation free of evaluation? If not, please give an example of an evaluation-free statement that matches the situation.

1. "One of the best ways to learn NVC is simply to practice, practice, practice."

2. "The boss is procrastinating around this decision."

3. "You lied to me about your grades."

4. "My husband hardly expresses any affection."

5. "You are arguing with me for the fourth time this week."

6. "Marshall said the only way to learn NVC is to practice, practice, practice."

7. "They made fun of the fact that I served pigs' feet for dinner."

8. "You drove the car without first getting my permission."

9. "They are destroying the environment."

10. "The doctor refuses to explain anything to me."

◎ Do the above exercise and the exercise in the book on your own.

Activity 2: Observing

Take a moment of silence to have everyone look around the room. Then ask each person to make an evaluation-laden observation, such as "People are looking tired," or "This room is cozy." Have the person pick someone else to make an evaluation-free observation of the same stimuli. (For "People are looking tired," the observation might be, "I saw three of us yawning during this exercise and another person rubbing her eyes.")

◎ Make two evaluation-laden observations about your current environment, and then restate them as observations free from evaluation.

Activity 3: Discussion

Take turns describing how you responded to the last item of the assignment (Individual Practice, #5). Have the group collectively discuss what they learned about observations and evaluations, including why we are practicing separating observations from evaluations.

◎ Write down your own thoughts on the value of practicing separating observations from evaluations.

Activity 4: Assignment Review

If there is time, share responses to the other pieces of the assignment. If time is running short, ask if anyone has questions regarding any other part of the assignment (including the Reading Review).

Three—Sample Responses to Leader's Guide

Responses for Alternative Activity 1:
Observation or Evaluation?

Sample observations free of evaluation to replace evaluation-laden observations:

NOTE: These are not examples of NVC, but only of the observation component.

---

1. "All the people in my practice group say that one of the best ways to learn NVC is simply to practice, practice, practice."

2. "The boss told us she would announce the decision by last week, but we still haven't heard."

3. "I heard you say you passed all your courses, but this report card shows two F's."

4. "My husband hasn't kissed me for two weeks."

5. "This is the fourth time this week that you stated you disagree with something I'm saying."

6. If the speaker actually heard Marshall say, "The only way to learn NVC is to practice, practice, practice," the speaker is stating what was heard without adding any evaluation.

7. "When I served pigs' feet for dinner, I heard laughter and someone saying, 'Where are the toenail clippers when we need them?'"

8. If both parties (e.g. parent and teenager in a family) are in clear agreement regarding what constitutes "first getting permission," then I would consider the speaker to be making an observation free of evaluation.

9. "They have clear cut over 90% of this territory, and are still continuing."

10. "The doctor did not say anything to me about what causes the pain or what can be done."

Review these sample responses, noticing how they are similar to or different from your own. What do you notice about these differences? How might you modify your own responses after reviewing these?

Exercises for the Chapter: Identifying and Expressing Feelings

Four—Individual Assignments

Reading Review

1. What is Rollo May referring to when he speaks of "symphony" vs. "bugle call"?

2. According to Marshall, what does American education focus on teaching students?

3. According to Marshall, why do people in certain careers have even more difficulty than the rest of us in identifying and expressing feelings?

4. What problems might a woman encounter if she "expresses feelings" by saying to her husband, "I feel like I'm living with a wall"?

5. What are advantages of expressing our feelings?

6. True or false: we are expressing a feeling whenever we begin a sentence with the words, "I feel . . ." Explain your answer.

7. Why does Marshall suggest that we identify specific emotions rather than depend upon expressions like "I feel good" and "I feel bad?"

Individual Practice

1. What are you feeling right now?

2. How do you know what you are feeling at any given moment? Where do you go to look?

3. Under the subheading "Feelings versus Non-feelings" in this Chapter, there are examples of words that tend to describe:

a. what we think we are (e.g. "I feel inadequate.")

b. how we think others are evaluating us (e.g. "I feel unimportant.")

c. how we think others are behaving towards or around us (e.g. "I feel misunderstood. I feel ignored.")

Think of five other words you might use that fall into these categories.

4. How do you feel in the presence of someone who does not express feelings?

5. It has been said that, except for grief, no feeling lasts longer than 40 seconds without changing. (Of course it may change back after a moment—depending on what new thoughts or circumstances arise.) What do you think? In the coming week, write down what you notice in one instance where you carefully watch and follow a specific feeling you are experiencing.

6. Imagine being given a choice to be born with or without feelings. Explain which you would choose and why.

7. Give three examples where you might use the expression "I feel," but in fact are expressing a thought rather than a feeling.

8. Start your own personal inventory of feelings.

a. Imagine all kinds of situations where life is going exactly the way you'd want. On a piece of paper, write down all the feelings you might feel in those situations.

b. Now imagine the kinds of situations where your needs are not being met, and list the feelings on another piece of paper.

c. Over the course of reading this book, challenge yourself to continually add to these lists as you build your symphony orchestra of feelings.

Four—Leader's Guide

Please remember that this guide is designed to serve you as the person who has offered to take responsibility to lead the next session. Use only those parts that support your plan for a fruitful and joyous session.

Activity 1: Noticing Feelings

Explain that the purpose of this activity is to help us notice our feelings in the moment and to see how they change from moment to moment. Each person, over the course of the evening, will give a signal to the group to signify: "Stop. Close your eyes. Go inside and find your feeling." Each person will decide when to give this signal by suddenly standing up in the middle of the circle without warning. It is not necessary for the person giving the signal to speak, and they can sit down again after they notice that the signal has been received by everyone.

> ◎ Take a moment to "Stop. Close Your Eyes. Go inside and identify your feeling."

Taking a minute of silence, each person looks inside to ask, "What do I feel right now? . . . And now? . . . And now?" It might be helpful for the leader to have a timer set on one minute, so they can participate without being interrupted to check the clock. At the end of the minute, the leader invites each person to name the feeling(s) they noticed and to share observations they made during the minute.

> ◎ While you're engaged in another activity, set a clock or watch to beep every 15 minutes for an hour. What are you feeling the moment the beeping sounds? Carefully observe and then record your feelings.

NOTE: Mention that the signals may be experienced as interruptions, especially for those who happen to be talking at the moment the signal arrives. Thus there may be feelings of irritation, frustration, etc. Ask everyone to notice those feelings and any thoughts that accompany them. Remind them that if they share why they feel a certain feeling, to try to acknowledge the underlying need. For example, rather than, "I feel irritated because I was interrupted," one might say, "I feel irritated because just as the signal came up I was wanting to get across an exciting idea—my need was to contribute."

 Notice interruptions you might experience other than the beeper you set. Try to identify if you feel differently about these unplanned interruptions and what needs are associated with these feelings.

After the round is completed, the leader will redirect attention to the person who had been speaking before the silence. It may be helpful during this session for everyone to have their "needs and feelings" lists handy. (See *Appendices 2 and 3*.)

Activity 2: Expressing Feelings

Lead the exercise Expressing Feelings, which is found in the book either at the end of the Chapter (Exercise 2) or at the end of the book (Practice 2). After completing the exercise, check the group's responses with Marshall's.

NOTE: If many people in your group have previously done this on their own, use the following alternative exercise.

 Try both these activities on your own. Record your responses in your notebook.

Alternative Activity 2: Expressing Feelings

In each of the following statements, do you regard the speaker to be expressing her or his feeling? If not, please play with the sentence until it does.

1. "I feel dismissed when no one at work responds to my suggestions."

2. "It feels completely incomprehensible how you can do such a thing."

3. "I'd be furious too if that had happened to me."

4. "You're wearing me out."

5. "I feel independent, now that I have my own car and paycheck."

6. "I am flabbergasted to see her picture on the front page."

7. "I feel you're annoying me on purpose."

8. "I feel displaced, with all this new technology coming in."

9. "I feel I am being unkind to them."

10. "I am feeling how disappointing it must be for her to see the house all empty now."

Activity 3: Review of Individual Practice

Go over the Individual Practice. Ask members to select pieces they most wish to cover, as there may not be time for the entire assignment. You may want to set time limits for discussions of #2, #4, #5, and #6.

Four—Sample Responses to Leader's Guide

Responses for Alternative Activity 2: Expressing Feelings

NOTE: These are not examples of NVC, but only of the feeling component.

---

1. "I feel *anxious* when no one at work responds to my suggestions."

2. "I feel very *puzzled* about how you could do such a thing."

3. "I feel *concerned* that this happened to you. I would have been furious if it had been me."

4. "I feel *exhausted*."

5. "I feel *pleased* and *proud* to have my own car and paycheck."

6. "*Flabbergasted*" expresses a feeling.

7. "I am *upset* because I think you are annoying me on purpose."

8. "I feel *worried* and *disheartened*, with all this new technology coming in."

9. "I feel *regret* around how I am behaving towards them."

10. "I am feeling *sad* thinking about how disappointed she must be to see the house all empty now."

◉ Review the previous sample responses. How are they similar to or different from your own? Review the list of words ("abandoned," "abused," etc.) under "Feelings versus Non-feelings" in Marshall's chapter to confirm that you have chosen words that express feelings rather than thoughts of how others are behaving towards you.

Exercises for the Chapter: Taking Responsibility for Our Feelings

5

Five—Individual Assignments

Reading Review

1. What is the difference between "stimulus" and "cause"?

2. What "causes" a particular feeling in us?

3. What are four options for hearing a difficult message?

4. How might we speak in a way that acknowledges responsibility for our feelings?

5. What is the basic mechanism behind guilt-tripping (getting someone to do something motivated by guilt)?

6. What phrase does Marshall suggest using as a way to increase awareness of our own responsibility for what we feel?

7. Instead of saying directly what we need, how do we often communicate to others when we want something? What kind of reaction are we likely to get by doing this?

8. How can we make it easier for other people to respond with compassion to what we want or are asking for?

9. Why might it be particularly difficult or painful for women to express needs?

10. What might be possible consequences of our not expressing our needs?

11. Define each of the three stages in emotional development that are mentioned in this chapter.

Individual Practice

1. Write the following:

   a. Briefly describe a situation where you experienced a distinct feeling,

   b. name the feeling,

   c. identify the stimulus, and

   d. identify the cause of the feeling.

2. In the situation you identified in #1 (above), give an example of how you might have responded using each of the four options.

3. Give an example of motivating someone else through the use of guilt, and explain how it might work.

4. Explain the difference between "taking responsibility" for someone else's feelings, and "compassionate caring" for them.

5. Give an example of each of the common speech patterns that tend to mask accountability for our own feelings:

   a. use of impersonal pronouns

   b. statements that mention only the actions of others

   c. use of the phrase "I feel (a feeling) because . . ." followed by a person or personal pronoun other than "I"

6. Take each example you gave under #5 (above) and change it by using the phrase, "I feel . . . because I . . ."

7. Identify a specific situation in your own life where your need for the following was not being met:

   a. autonomy

   b. celebration

   c. integrity

   d. understanding from others

   e. understanding of others

   f. community

   g. peace

8. While the three stages of emotional development are described as a linear progression, many of us may experience ourselves waffling back and forth as we continue to grow in consciousness and emotional maturity. Can you recall situations in your own life to illustrate each of the three stages?

Five—Leader's Guide

Activity 1: Four Options for Hearing a Negative Message

This activity calls for five participants. One person will make up a "difficult to hear" statement, such as, "It's really objectionable the way you constantly impose your views on everyone else!" She will express this statement with feeling, repeating it to each of the other four participants.

Each of the other four selects a different option to hear that message. Each will express out loud a thought that reflects the particular option he or she had chosen.

Example:

Option 1: A person who hears blame and blames self might express the following thought out loud to the group: "Oh, gosh, I am so controlling! I'm acting just like my mother. No wonder people find me objectionable."

Option 2: A person who hears blame and blames the speaker might have the following thought: "Yeah right, if the idiot bothered to listen, he'd realize that everyone else in the room just happens to agree with me!"

Option 3: A person who focuses attention on his or her own feelings and needs might express the following: "Sigh . . . I feel sad because I would like more understanding for how I am trying to help here."

Option 4: A person who focuses attention on the feelings and needs of the speaker might have the following thought: "Hmm . . . I wonder if he is irritated because he wants everyone's views to be heard and considered. . . . "

After the five people have completed the first round, rotate roles. If necessary, adjust this activity to accommodate groups larger or smaller than five. Ideally each participant gets an opportunity to practice each of the five roles.

Note: For this activity, it is helpful to create a set of five large cards with the following words on each:
- (first card) Difficult to hear message
- (second card) Option One: Hears blame and blames self
- (third card) Option Two: Hears blame and blames other
- (fourth card) Option Three: Senses own feelings and needs
- (fifth card) Option Four: Senses other's feelings and needs

Give one to each of the five participants and rotate cards at the end of each round.

◉ Try this on your own, making up your own statement and the four alternative responses. Record your responses in your notebook.

Activity 2: "What is my need here?"

A. Guide the group through this exercise with everyone taking turns reading an item out loud and identifying possible needs.

Begin with the question, "What might be my need if I had the following thought in my head during a meeting?"

1. "She's irresponsible: We all agreed to let someone know if we weren't going to show up."

2. "Everyone else here knows more NVC than I do."

3. "That's totally irresponsible, what he just said!"

4. "She always takes more time than anyone else."

5. "People needing therapy ought to get professional help. We can't handle that level of dysfunctionality here!"

6. "This is boring."

7. "There should be a rule against using offensive sexist language in a group like this."

8. "I hope my voice doesn't start shaking."

9. "There he goes again . . . I wish someone would shut him up!"

10. "Wait until next week when it's my turn to be leader: I'll interrupt her just like she squashed me. Let's see how she'll like it then!"

11. "This group of people is so cold and rigid."

12. "This is the third time he's disrupted our opening circle by arriving late."

13. "All this head talk drives me crazy."

14. "I can't stand the way they're being so sweet. Don't they realize NVC is not about being nice?"

15. "Hello, hello, we're supposed to be speaking NVC at an NVC practice group, yeah, duh!"

16. "It disgusts me when people don't prepare for these meetings and just expect those of us who did our homework to supply the answers."

◎ Try this on your own. Record your responses in your notebook.

B. Now have people take turns translating each statement into a possible observation, feeling, and need. Example #1. *"She's irresponsible: we all agreed to let someone know if we weren't going to show up."* Translation: *"When I hear that none of us got a call from her, I feel discouraged because I want to be able to count on us carrying through with agreements we make together."* (Universal needs: reliability, trust, integrity.)

◎ Try listening to a television show or movie and identifying the needs of the characters when they make statements like these. Record your responses in your notebook.

Five–Sample Responses to Leader's Guide

Responses for Activity 2A: "What is my need here?"

1. reliability, respect, consideration

2. competence, acceptance, respect

3. understanding, empathy, honesty

4. mutuality, consideration, efficiency

5. safety, integrity, competence

6. stimulation, purpose, challenge

7. respect, community, support

8. acceptance, competence, effectiveness

9. consideration, connection, stimulation

10. empathy, appreciation, support

11. inclusion, warmth, community

12. cooperation, respect, order

13. connection, meaning, authenticity

14. authenticity, connection, understanding

15. cooperation, dependability, connection

16. mutuality, appreciation, support

◉ Review these sample responses, noticing how they are similar to or different from your own. What do you notice about these differences? How might you modify your own responses after reviewing these?

Responses for Activity 2B: Translating

1. "When I hear that none of us has received a call from her saying she'd be absent, I feel disappointed because I have a need to rely on agreements being kept."

2. "When I see you all expressing needs so quickly, I feel anxious because I want to be more competent. I'm also nervous because I am hoping to be accepted in this group."

3. "When I hear him say he's not responsible for what happened, I feel aggravated because I want to be understood better and to receive some empathy."

4. "When I recall how long she took to answer the last question, I feel impatient because I would like to use group time more efficiently."

5. "After watching that last interaction, I feel really worried because I want peoples' emotional needs to be well attended to, and I am not confident that we have the skills to do that here."

6. "When I hear the trainer explaining the process, I feel bored, because I need to learn something new."

7. "When I hear words like that used in this group, I feel hurt because I value respect and would like more consideration for how some of us may be affected by hearing these expressions."

8. "When I remember my voice sometimes shakes when I get nervous, I feel even more nervous because I want to be able to communicate effectively and be understood."

9. "When I see him open his mouth again, I feel exasperated, because I want there to be equal opportunity for everyone to talk."

10. "When she speaks before I'm finished, I feel hurt, because I am wanting more support for the effort I am making to lead the group."

11. "When I don't see anyone greeting the new people, I feel uneasy because I value a welcoming and inclusive space."

12. "When I see him arrive late for the third time during opening circle, I feel irritated because I would like to see more consideration of how it affects the flow of what we are doing."

13. "When I listen to what you are saying, I feel confused and exhausted because I am wanting there to be connection and understanding between us on a heart level."

14. "When I hear the dozens of compliments, praise and positive judgments over the course of the evening, I feel annoyed because I yearn for authentic connection."

15. "When I hear so many evaluations in our conversation, I feel concerned because I want us to spend our time purposefully, practicing NVC, and relating to each other with honesty and empathy."

16. "When I see the same three people having done their homework, I feel disgusted because I want equal participation and sharing of the work."

Review these sample responses, noticing how they are similar to or different from your own. Do you recognize cases where the feelings and needs words used in these samples more closely match those in the book than the ones you chose? What do you notice about these differences? When you notice these differences write down how you feel and what you may need in relation to having different answers than those given here.

Exercises for the Chapter: Requesting That Which Would Enrich Life

Six—Individual Assignments

Reading Review

1. What constitutes a "request" in NVC? What is its purpose? How do we express it? How is it different from a demand? How might we "test" whether it is a demand or a request?

2. What is likely to happen when we:

   a. express requests in vague and abstract language?

   b. express what we are wanting by only stating our feelings?

3. Why do we sometimes hear a demand even when the speaker is actually making a request of us?

4. The author believes that whenever we speak to someone, we are requesting something in return. List three things we may want in return.

5. What's the reason to ask someone to reflect back what we just said to them?

6. What might we do if the other person gets annoyed when we ask for a reflection?

7. When speaking in a group, why is it important to be clear about what we want back?

8. Why does Marshall mention the Indian custom of saying "bas?"

9. What is the objective for using NVC? Are there situations for which NVC is not designed?

10. List some common words that are expressive of (or associated with) demands.

Individual Practice

1. Recall an interaction with someone that did not satisfy you. Give one or several requests you made or could have made in this situation using positive action language.

2. For the same situation above, write down how you would tell the other person your observation, feeling, and need. Then follow with:

   a. a request for what the listener is feeling, and

   b. a request for what the listener is thinking.

3. What might you do to strengthen your consciousness of what you want back when you talk to others?

4. Write down the words you might use to request someone to reflect back what you just told them.

5. Write down what you might say if the other person (#4, above) responds with, "It's such a pain talking to you—all this repeating back. You treat me like I'm an idiot."

6. Recall something you said (or can imagine yourself saying) at a meeting or in a group. Did you make clear what you wanted back? If not, how could you have done so?

7. Recall a specific situation when you asked something of someone. Was it a request or a demand? How do you know?

8. Notice, when you are talking to yourself, whether you demand or request. Give examples.

Six—Leader's Guide

1. It may be helpful to remind your group that though we are empha-sizing "requests" in this session, they constitute only one compo-nent of the NVC process, the purpose of which is to inspire heart connection between ourselves and others. Specifying the behavior we are requesting is important for getting our needs met: however, just because a request is "perfectly formulated" does not mean that it will inspire the requested behavior. We want to stay grounded in the need that we are seeking to fulfill, and to remember there are many ways (many different requests, behaviors, strategies, and solutions) to meet that need.

2. If we engage in an "NVC dance" (respectful dialogue) with the other, the "solution" (or "agreed-on behaviors") that emerges out of the open heart space that connects us may bear absolutely no resemblance to the original request we made of the other person. Let's think of using requests in NVC to continue the dance, not as a test of our success in getting what we want. Remember also the two common NVC requests: 1) for empathy, "Would you be will-ing to tell me what you just heard me say?" and 2) for honesty, "Would you be willing to tell me what you are feeling when you hear me say this?" or, "Would you be willing to tell me what you think about (some specific item) I just said?"

Activity 1: Incorporating All Four Components into Formal NVC

Imagine situations where someone utters the following statements. In each case, translate the statement using all four components of "formal NVC," paying special attention that the request is positive, concrete, and immediately do-able.

1. "Your dog just made a mess on my lawn." (Translate to: "When I see your dog . . . [observation], I feel . . . [feeling] because I need . . . [need], and would you be willing to . . . [request]?")

2. "Yelling obscenities isn't going to get you what you want."

3. "By putting your money in mutual funds, you're just supporting guns and tobacco and sweat shops and all the things we're trying to change in this world."

4. "This soup is much too caloric."

5. "At this company, we require teamwork. If that's not a priority for you, you'd better be looking for another job."

6. "Hey, kids, flashlights aren't toys. Don't waste batteries. They cost money."

7. "Where in the world do you think you are going in the middle of the school day?"

8. "But you told me two weeks ago that it would be fine if I were to take a long weekend this month."

9. "Honey, the baby just threw up."

10. "That's not NVC—what you just said."

⊚ Try this on your own. Record your responses in your notebook.

Activity 2: Requests to Meet Needs

Give your group a silent minute for everyone to think of a situation in their lives where some need is not being met. Ask them to formulate a request (of themselves or of another party) that addresses the unmet need.

Each person then:

1. presents her or his request in the form of a direct quote, e.g. *"Would you be willing to _____"* and

2. states (very briefly—no more than 1-2 sentences) the situation if it is not clear to the rest of the group. Make sure everyone in the

group agrees that the request is positive and immediately do-able before moving on to the next person.

 Try this on your own. Record your responses in your notebook. Place yourself in the position of someone hearing your request. Ask yourself, "If I heard this request, would I know what specific action I am being asked to take, and when to take it?"

Six—Sample Responses to Leader's Guide

Responses for Activity 1: Incorporating All Four Components into Formal NVC

1. "When I see your dog leaving turds on the lawn, I feel upset. We have kids who play here and I want the yard to be a safe, clean space for them. Would you be willing to use this plastic bag to remove the turds?"

2. "When I hear you addressing me like that, I feel agitated because I need cooperation and a peaceful resolution of our differences. Are you willing to tell me what you are feeling and needing right now instead of what you think I am?"

3. "When I hear you have put your money in mutual funds, I feel dejected because I'd like to see us put our resources into what we value, rather than to support guns, tobacco, and sweatshops. Would you be willing to tell me what you are feeling when you hear me say this?"

4. "I am worried about the calories in this soup because I really need to take care of my health. Would you be willing to give me a bowl of noodles instead?"

5. "When I read this report you wrote, I feel troubled, because I value teamwork and I need some reassurance that we are on the same page. Would you be willing to make an appointment so we can discuss how we each see the priorities for this job?"

6. "When I see you kids playing with the flashlights under the blanket, I feel uneasy. I want these flashlights to last so they'll be available if we have an emergency. Would you be willing to put them away?"

7. "When I see you walking out of school in the middle of the day, I feel alarmed. I need some understanding here. Are you willing to explain to me where you are headed?"

8. "When I hear you say 'no' to my taking a long weekend this month and then remember your saying two weeks ago that it would be fine, I feel frustrated and confused. I need more clarity and some reassurance that we are communicating accurately. Would you be willing to tell me what you just heard me say?"

9. "When I see the baby throw up, I feel . . . uh . . . disgusted, because I value a healthy and pleasing environment. Would you be willing to wipe up the barf?"

10. "When I hear you refer to me as 'overbearing,' I feel exasperated because I need to be understood. Would you be willing to first tell me what I'm doing or saying that leads you to perceive me as 'over-bearing?'"

Review these sample responses, noticing how they are similar to or different from your own. What do you notice about these differences? How might you modify your own responses after reviewing these?

Exercises for the Chapter: Receiving Empathically

Seven—Individual Assignments

Reading Review

1. What are the "two parts" and "four components" of NVC?

2. What is empathy?

3. What mental condition is required of us in order to extend empathy towards another person?

4. Instead of offering empathy, what are some other ways people tend to respond when they hear someone expressing pain or dissatisfaction?

5. Why did Marshall's daughter slam the door in his face after he told her she was gorgeous?

6. What is the difference between empathy and an intellectual understanding of someone?

7. What is the difference between sympathy and empathy?

8. In NVC, as we receive other people's words, what are we especially listening for?

9. Why does Marshall encourage the use of the phrase, "Are you feeling unhappy because you . . . ?"

10. When people are expressing displeasure towards you, what is the advantage of listening for what they need rather than what they are thinking?

11. What purpose(s) does paraphrasing serve?

12. What does paraphrasing in NVC consist of?

13. What is the difference between NVC paraphrasing and direct questioning? What is the advantage of paraphrasing?

14. If you were experiencing strong emotions and wanting to ask direct questions of someone, what does Marshall suggest doing first? Why?

15. Under what circumstances would you paraphrase or refrain from paraphrasing what someone is saying to you?

16. If people react negatively to our paraphrasing their words, what might we do?

17. Why does Marshall caution us against proceeding quickly towards helping people solve the problems they bring to us?

18. How do we know when a person has received adequate empathy and is ready to move on?

19. What prevents us from offering empathy to someone who is in pain?

20. What can we do when we know that the other person needs empathy, but we ourselves are hurting too much to offer any? Describe three or four alternatives.

Individual Practice

1. Recall an experience you had of "listen(ing) to someone with (your) whole being."

2. What are some conditions—either internal (inside yourself) or external—that support your ability to be empathic? What are conditions that work against it?

3. Describe two experiences where you were expressing some pain to somebody, and then got back one of the common behaviors identified by Holley Humphrey (under subheading "Presence: don't just do something: stand there" in this Chapter). In each case, did you enjoy the response you received? Why or why not?

4. Go over the list of common behaviors (the list of "doo-doos," i.e. things we tend to "do" rather than be empathic). Which ones are particularly familiar to you? Recall two situations where you responded with a doo-doo. Briefly write out a 2-line dialogue for each situation:

   a. what the person said (expressing their pain)

   b. what you said in response (name the behavior)

5. Now go back to what you wrote under b. above and change it into a verbalized empathic response. (In real life, of course, your empathy may be silent.) Remember that empathy entails sensing or guessing, rather than knowing, the other person's feelings and needs. In offering verbal empathy, we take the risk of guessing incorrectly, with the hope that the response to our incorrect guess will lead us closer to an accurate understanding.

6. Return to the two situations you described in #3 (above), and in each case imagine an empathic response you would have enjoyed receiving from the person to whom you had expressed your pain.

7. Describe a situation where you would choose to reflect back someone's words. Describe a situation where you would choose not to reflect back. Why the difference?

8. Marshall quotes Joseph Campbell as saying, "'What will they think of me?' must be put aside for bliss," and then writes, "We begin to feel this bliss when messages previously experienced as critical or blaming begin to be seen for the gifts they are: opportunities to give to people who are in pain."

   Are you able to recall a situation where your ability to hear the feeling and need behind a seemingly harsh or difficult message opened the way to happiness—to being able to exercise your power to contribute to someone's well being?

9. What would you like your intention to be when you reflect back someone's words? How might you ascertain that this is your intention in a specific situation?

◎ Reflect on all the words you utter and release into the world, and what the intention is behind each of them. What can you do to increase your awareness of whether the intention is or is not in keeping with NVC?

Seven—Leader's Guide

You have now learned both parts and all four components of the NVC process. From here on group activities may consist of role-play (See *Practicing Together, K*), empathy-sessions (See *Practicing Together, J*), and live group interactions (see *Practicing Together, I*) as well as more structured practice to review the basics of the process.

Activity 1: Short Empathy Exercises

Following are six short exercises on empathy. If you also go over members' responses to Part II of the assignment, there may not be much time left for other activities.

1. Someone at work says to you:
    "I couldn't sleep until 3 a.m. last night, thinking about our presentation today. So this morning I figured I'd better drink lots of coffee to keep me awake and alert . . . but now my head is killing me! Why do I always get hit with headaches when something important needs to be done!?"

    a. Give a reply that demonstrates intellectual understanding of the situation by addressing the speaker's question (last sentence).

    b. Give a reply that demonstrates sympathy.

    c. Give a reply that offers advice.

    d. Give a reply verbalizing empathy.

2. At a meeting, while you are in the middle of a sentence, someone turns to you suddenly and says, "Don't you ever let someone else have a chance to talk?" Respond to this person with empathy by:

    a. sensing and reflecting back what the person might be observing

    b. sensing and reflecting back what the person might be feeling and needing

    c. sensing and reflecting back what the person might be requesting

3. The following dialogue takes place between two persons who share a house:

Housemate A: *"You never remember to turn off the lights."*

Housemate B: *"You're irritated and would like more awareness about how we use resources . . ."*

Have two people read the above exchange out loud. Now have everyone take the role of Housemate B and repeat the words out loud in the following ways:

a. with a little edge of sarcasm

b. in a declarative way

c. in an empathic (sensing) way

Briefly discuss what people noticed while using the different tones of voice.

4. Recall a situation where you and another person are upset at each other. You are aware that you are too upset to be able to offer empathy to the other person.

a. Write down what you might say to the other person if you choose to "scream in NVC." (If necessary, refer to the author's story of "screaming nonviolently" at the end of this Chapter in the book.)

b. Write down what you might say to yourself if you choose to give yourself emergency first aid empathy.

5. Suppose you wanted someone to paraphrase your words back to you, but you are sensing a little resistance on their part. What might you say to them?

6. Do a short role-play between yourself (a person using NVC) and a person who remarks: "I know you want us to reflect back what we say and all that, but we have an agenda here. We have work to do. We can't spend all day yakking, you know."

Try this on your own. Record your responses in your notebook.

Seven—Sample Responses to Leader's Guide

Responses for Activity 1: Short Empathy Exercises

1. Sample responses

   a. "It's probably because you have a lot of tension when you are anticipating something important. Or maybe it's a combination of stress, lack of sleep, and the caffeine that's causing your headache."

   b. "I really feel for you. It's the worst thing to have a horrible headache when you are about to do an important presentation!"

   c. "Why don't you take this ice pack and lie down for about 10 minutes?"

   d. "Are you frustrated because you would really like to be feeling energetic, healthy, and clear-headed for this presentation?"

2. Sample responses

   a. "Are you referring to my going, 'Oh no, oh no, oh no' when Peter pointed to the map?"

   b. "Are you feeling irritated because you want everyone to be heard?"

   c. "Would you like for us to go around and hear from everyone before I speak again?"

3. No written response

4. Sample responses

   a. "Stop! Stop, please stop! I need help! I want to be able to hear you, but I am much, much too upset right now to be able to do that. I feel desperate! I need us to slow down! Can you tell me what you are hearing me say here?"

   b. "**She's crazy!**—Oh, self-empathy . . . I am shocked hearing her response, really shocked . . . and I need . . . need . . . to understand, first to understand why she did what she did. It makes no sense—I am perplexed, puzzled. I need clarity, and I am also feeling really, really, really, really, really upset . . . sad, I feel sad, sad and disappointed. I had dreams of us working together, teaming up, and supporting each other. I want to be able to trust—I thought we had agreed. I am confused and sad and hurt . . . I want to understand why she did it and I want her to understand me."

5. "I realize it might seem a bit awkward in the beginning, but I would really appreciate your telling me back what you hear me say. It's important for me to know that I've communicated myself accurately, because our connection means a lot to me."

6. Sample responses

1st Person: *I know you want us reflecting back what we say and all that, but we have an agenda here. We have work to do. We can't spend all day yakking, you know.*

2nd Person (using NVC): *Sounds like you want to make sure that we complete what we've set out to do?*

1st Person: *You bet. There's a lot we need to cover today to come up with some clear decisions.*

2nd Person (using NVC): *Are you feeling a bit anxious and needing reassurance that our discussions here will be efficient and clear?*

1st Person: *Exactly.*

2nd Person (using NVC): *I appreciate hearing you say that. I have the same need, and I would be more confident in its being met if we would reflect back what one person said before another person speaks. Would you be willing to try that?*

◎ Review these sample responses, noticing how they are similar to or different from your own. What do you notice about these differences? How might you modify your own responses after reviewing these?

Exercises for the Chapter: The Power of Empathy

8

Eight—Individual Assignments

Reading Review

1. What do the father of humanistic psychology, Carl Rogers, and Milly, the elementary school student, understand in common?

2. Under what circumstances are we most hesitant to express vulnerability (i.e. to let others see what's really going on for us)? What might we do in those circumstances?

3. Why is it so important to be able to empathize with someone who says "no" to you?

4. Why are we warned against putting our "but" in the face of an angry person?

5. According to the author, why do conversations drag or go dead? What are ways to revive them?

6. For many of us, "interrupting" is a social taboo. What gives the author the courage to interrupt someone in the middle of a sentence?

7. What might we do in the presence of someone who will neither talk nor respond to our questions?

Individual Practice

1. Bring to mind two situations where you experienced conflict—one with someone whom you regard as a "superior" (for example, an authority figure) and the other with someone who is subordinate or dependent upon you in some way (a child, someone working for you, etc.) What would you say to empathize with each of them? Do you notice any difference

in the ease (or difficulty) with which you can empathize with them?

2. The Cleveland gang members laughed at the author in a mocking way, "Oh, look, he's feeling hurt—isn't that too bad!" Write down how the author might have responded using each of the four options in hearing a difficult message; in other words, what might he have said if he had:

   a. blamed himself,

   b. blamed the others,

   c. sensed his own feelings and needs, or

   d. sensed the feelings and needs of the others.

3. Recall a situation where you perceived someone as having fun laughing at or mocking you, taking pleasure in your pain, or bullying or being vengeful with the intention to cause you hurt.

   a. Take time to be with whatever feelings and sensations arise in you as you re-create this situation.

   b. What feelings and needs are you aware of? (There may be many.)

4. Can you recall a situation where you were having fun laughing at someone else, taking pleasure in their pain, or intending to cause them hurt? If so, empathize with how you were feeling at that moment. What were your feelings in addition to the apparent enjoyment you might have been taking in seeing the person in pain? What were your met and unmet needs?

5. Return to the situation that was evoked in #3. This time, see if you are able to empathize with the other person by sensing what feelings and needs might have been stirring in them even as they appeared happy to see you hurting.

6. Why do you think it is often easier to empathize with a stranger or someone we don't know well than it is to empathize with those who are closest to us?

7. Practice translating "no" into "yes." When we say "no" to something, we are actually saying "yes" to something else, e.g. "Behind my "no"

to going out for ice cream is my "yes" to staying in a place where I feel safe." Recall two or three instances when you said "no" to someone. What was the "yes" behind your "no"? Use positive language to express what you wanted or needed.

8. Do you recall an instance when you felt bored talking with someone? If so, write down what you might have said at that instance by using Nonviolent Communication. Give two other examples of something you might have said in that instance to bring the conversation to life.

9. Imagine or recall a situation where the other person neither talks to you nor responds to your questions.

   a. What might you be feeling and needing?

   b. What might the other person be feeling or needing?

   c. How might you express your empathy in this situation for the other person?

   d. How might you express it for yourself?

10. Go over the table on page 117, *Translating Judgments Into Self-empathy*

   a. A woman is listening to the statement at the top of the table. (These words are the "Stimulus.")

   b. She hears blame and criticism, and her thoughts turn to "what's wrong with him." ("Life-alienating Thoughts"–left-hand column)

   c. Becoming aware of her own thoughts, she recognizes that she is in pain. She then makes a conscious effort to translate the thoughts into "Self-empathy." (Right-hand column) She knows there is a much higher chance that her needs will be met if she focuses on her needs rather than on "what's wrong with him."

   This example of what the woman might say to herself when translating her habitual ways of thinking does not capture the essence of self-empathy, which is non-verbal. Self-empathy requires us to stop and *be* fully present to our internal experience. It is not *thinking* about what we are feeling. It is *feeling* what we are feeling and being open to whatever flood of sensations is present without either shrinking from it, trying to change it, or going up to our heads with it. It is not about successfully identifying our unmet need with the accurate word, but fully sensing the yearning of that unfulfilled need inside of us. Self-empathy is not a quick fix. It is a process that may take time, and when allowed to come to completion, will lead to a shift in our experience, a deepening, and a release.

NOTE: There is sometimes the concern of "wallowing" or "indulging" in feelings that we consider to be "negative." We may be fearful that by paying attention to these feelings, we are feeding them. Self-empathy is full presence and acceptance of whatever feelings exist without either pushing them away (denying) or hanging on to them (prolonging).

Our tendency is to avoid feelings that are unpleasant even though we may intellectually know, "You have to feel it to heal it." "Wallowing" is not being present to our feelings, but consists of prolonged thinking about them or about the circumstances that triggered us. Each of us needs to experiment and discover the nature of "presence," of being present to feelings as opposed to denying or indulging in them.

---

11. Take a situation where an external stimulus triggered habitual ways of thinking in you.

    a. Write down the stimulus in the form of an observation without evaluation.

    b. Write down the life-alienating thoughts stimulated by this observation.

    c. Translate these thoughts: What are you feeling, and what are the unfulfilled needs behind those thoughts? Allow yourself time to sit silently with whatever feelings and needs come up. Notice what happens as you allow yourself to be fully present to yourself, to your own internal experience. Notice any flux in sensations and emotions and any mental commentaries.

    d. When you decide you are complete with this process, write down the feelings and needs you explored and anything else you noticed that made an impression on you.

TRANSLATING JUDGMENTS INTO SELF-EMPATHY

Stimulus:

I can't believe your mother took that fall a year ago and you never bothered to verify whether she'd broken any bones. You should've just taken her down to the States for an X-ray. It would've been easy and she would've been fine today. You shouldn't just let things slide like that. Now she's never going to walk again.

Life-alienating Thoughts:	Self-empathy:
What an insensitive jerk!	*Upset . . . I am just so upset to hear him talk to me in that way . . . at a time when I feel vulnerable, I need compassion, and I want to hear some caring words!*
He's totally rude. What gives him the right to tell me what to do?	*Uh . . . mmm, what's my feeling here? I'm feeling warm, my neck feels tight, I feel, yeah . . . annoyed, annoyed, here's a constriction in my chest, ooh . . . tension . . . I'm saying "he's rude"—I'm sensing I want respect, I want more acceptance in how I might have chosen to do things.*
The guy's mouthing off without the faintest idea of what I went through trying to get that X-ray! He is a very ignorant man.	*I feel so much hurt. I'm sad. He doesn't know what happened. I have a need to be understood. I want acknowledgment for all those challenges, difficulties. I want to be seen and understood accurately!*

Eight—Leader's Guide

Announce an intention to devote this session fully to the awareness and practice of empathy from the first hello to the last goodbye. What form would our world take if every one of us took time to practice the intention of responding to each other and to ourselves with empathy? Imagine having two-and-a-half hours to share a taste of that world together!

Use any or a combination of the following activities to focus today's practice on empathy:

- a. Spontaneous live empathic interactions among members of the circle

- b. Empathy sessions (Refer to *Practicing Together, J*)

- c. Sharing your responses to Individual Practice

- d. Any of the following structured practices and exercises on empathy:

Activity 1: Empathic Dialogue

Take the dialogue from the detox center and continue on with at least two more exchanges. Imagine the woman staying present in her empathy during this life-threatening moment.

- a. Man: *Give me a room.*

- b. Woman: *All the rooms are filled already.*

- c. Man (with knife poised across her throat): *You bitch, don't lie to me! You do too have a room!*

- d. Woman: *It sounds like you're really angry and you want to be given a room.*

- e. Man: *I may be an addict, but by God, I deserve respect. I'm tired of nobody giving me respect. My parents don't give me respect. I'm gonna get respect!*

- f. Woman: *Are you fed up, not getting the respect that you want?*

- g. Man: _____

h. Woman: _____

i. Man: _____

j. Woman: _____

◎ Complete the dialogue g, h, i, and j (above) on your own. Record your responses in your notebook.

Activity 2: Practice Expressing Empathy

Practice expressing empathy towards someone who makes the following statements. Use the format, "Do you feel x . . . because you need y . . .?"

a. "The people I cook for are really picky."

b. "Be quiet!"

c. "You wouldn't say things like that if you loved your country."

d. "My parents never tell me the truth anyway."

e. "I can't stand the way you always contradict me."

◎ Try this on your own. Record your responses in your notebook.

Activity 3: Empathy Role-play

A person begins the role-play by taking one of the following lines. Others in the circle empathize, and the person continues the dialogue until she or he is satisfied with having been fully heard. Remember: "Empathy before education." Avoid problem solving and giving advice until the speaker has received adequate empathy.

a. "I don't know what to do with people in my life who just adamantly refuse to hear what I am saying."

b. "When someone calls me a name, I am in pain, but then I also realize that they are in pain to be calling me a name in the first place. What am I to do?"

c. "When I catch myself blaming someone who obviously needs empathy, and I watch my heart closing down, I end up blaming myself. That's not helpful, is it?"

d. "Ever since I've begun using NVC, people have been taking advantage of me. My co-workers, the building manager, even my kids—they all push me around just because they know they can get away with it now."

◎ Practice expressing empathy with friends or family members who express strong needs and feelings. Or try watching a television show or movie and empathizing with the feelings and needs of the characters. Record your responses in your notebook.

Eight—Sample Responses to Leader's Guide

Responses for Activity 1: Empathic Dialogue

1. Man: *Yes, I am! Fed up! Sick and tired! I'm not gonna take it any more!*

2. Woman: *Sounds like you are really determined to protect yourself and get the respect you need.*

3. Man: *Yeah, yeah, that's right. Nobody knows what it feels like . . . They force me to beg for everything—a bit of food, a place to stay . . .*

4. Woman: *Do you feel frustrated, and would you like more understanding for how painful it is to be in your situation?*

> ◎ Review these sample responses, noticing how they are similar to or different from your own. What do you notice about these differences? How might you modify your own responses after reviewing these?

Responses for Activity 2: Expressing empathy

1. "Are you feeling disheartened because you need appreciation?"

2. "Are you feeling annoyed because you need respect?"

3. "Are you feeling agitated because you need to trust that there is support for the country?" (Or: "Do you feel agitated because you value support and community?")

4. "Are you feeling discouraged because you need honesty and connection?"

5. "Are you feeling frustrated because you need harmony?"

> ◎ Review these sample responses, noticing how they are similar to or different from your own. What do you notice about these differences? How might you modify your own responses after reviewing these?

Exercises for the Chapter: Connecting Compassionately with Ourselves

9

NOTE: This chapter doesn't exist in the first edition of the book. Some of the topics addressed here were addressed in the chapter Liberating Ourselves and Counseling Others in the first edition. If you have an early edition of the book you may wish to skip this assignment and return to it only after completing the chapter Liberating Ourselves and Counseling Others and its workbook assignments.

Nine—Individual Assignments

Reading Review

1. Why does Marshall emphasize the importance of using NVC with ourselves?

2. What is lost when we forget the "subtle, sneaky, important reason" why we were born "a human being and not a chair?"

3. How do people tend to evaluate themselves when they are unhappy with what they have done?

4. Why does Marshall wish to avoid self-judgment as a pathway to growth, learning, and change?

5. How are others likely to respond when they sense shame or guilt behind our kindness towards them?

6. Why does Marshall consider "should" to be a "violent" word?

7. Repeatedly declaring what we "must" do may actually prevent us from doing it. Why?

8. According to NVC, what are we really saying if we imply that someone is wrong or bad?

9. What are the two aspects of self-evaluation that Marshall emphasizes and values?

10. What are we likely to feel when we criticize ourselves for "messing up"?

11. What happens to us when we get connected to the unmet need behind self-criticism?

12. Describe the process of NVC mourning and self-forgiveness.

13. What are the two parts of ourselves that we hold empathically when we are being compassionate with ourselves?

14. What are the three steps to translating a language of "have to" to a language of "choose to?"

15. What is the purpose of such translation?

16. Under what circumstance might hard work, challenge, and frustration still be experienced as "play?"

17. What are two examples of extrinsic reward?

18. What are the disadvantages to being motivated by extrinsic reward?

19. What does Marshall consider to be the most socially dangerous way that we behave when we're cut off from our needs? Why?

Individual Practice

1. Mourning in Giraffe.
   This is a process to heal ourselves concerning a choice we made in the past that we now regret. It is a way of acknowledging our regret and of

empathizing with ourselves so we can grow beyond our past limitations.

Perhaps we may think we are "correcting the situation" or "making up" for a past mistake by continuing to blame ourselves and prolonging our sense of guilt and shame. Yet, as St. Frances de Sales wrote, "Those who are fretted by their own failings will not correct them. All profitable corrections come from a calm and peaceful mind."

There is a belief in our culture that the suffering of the perpetrator makes up for the loss that victims undergo—an eye for an eye. As a practitioner of NVC, if I lose an eye as a consequence of your behavior, I know my deep need for empathy, compassion, safety, etc., will not be met by your offering me either your self-judgment or your eye. I will be able to receive what I need from you only after you have taken the much harder path of truly mourning the choices you have made. The healing between us will happen when I can hear the depth of your mourning and you can offer me the depth of empathy that I need.

Use the flow chart on the following page to mourn a choice you made in the past that you now regret.

a. Observation: what I said or did in the past that I now regret

b. Self-judgments: what I think of myself for having done or said (a)

c. Current feelings and needs: translate self-judgments into feelings and needs

d. Empathy for myself: determine what need I was trying to fulfill when I chose to take the action or say the words I now regret

e. Current request of myself:

Aware of my current feelings and unfulfilled needs (c), I would like to address my needs (d) in this manner

MOURNING: HEALING THE PAST©

Recall something you did or said in the past which you now wish you had not. Words in ovals refer to the past; words in the rectangles refer to the present

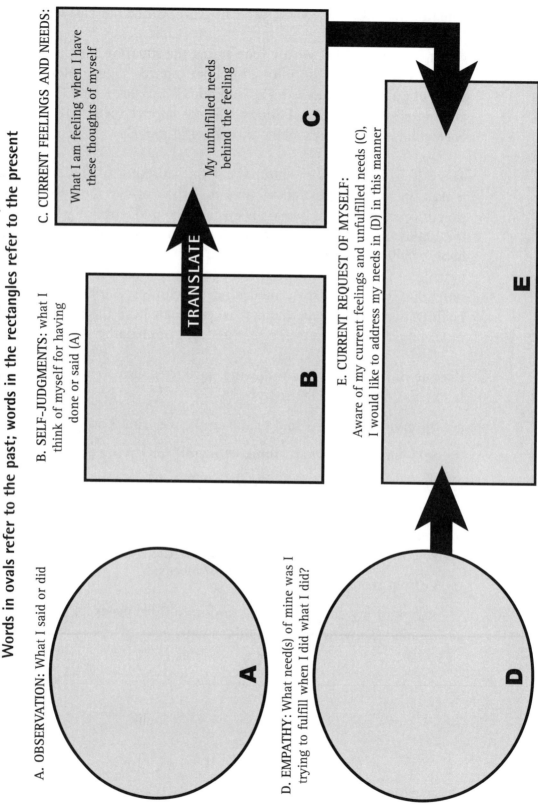

A. OBSERVATION: What I said or did

A

B. SELF-JUDGMENTS: what I think of myself for having done or said (A)

B

TRANSLATE

C. CURRENT FEELINGS AND NEEDS:

What I am feeling when I have these thoughts of myself

My unfulfilled needs behind the feeling

C

D. EMPATHY: What need(s) of mine was I trying to fulfill when I did what I did?

D

E. CURRENT REQUEST OF MYSELF:
Aware of my current feelings and unfulfilled needs (C), I would like to address my needs in (D) in this manner

E

2. Translating "have to" to "choose to"

Make a list of all the things that you don't like doing, but see yourself as having to do anyway. Use the following format:

"I have to _____ (fill in task).*"*

Translate each item into the statement:

"I choose to _____ (fill in the task above) *because I want* _____ (fill in what you value, need, or want).*"*

3. Think of ways in which you try to acquire money in your life as strategies you have chosen to meet certain needs. List the needs. Imagine at least one other possible strategy for meeting each of the needs you named.

Example:

I try to acquire money by asking my brother for the $25 he had agreed would be his share for the birthday present I got our mother last month.

My needs:

    a. equity and balance—*I want equal contribution from us towards supporting the well-being of our mother.*

    b. reliability—*I want to know I can count on agreements being followed through.*

    c. connection—*I want to re-connect with my ex-girlfriend by offering to take her out to lunch.*

Other possible strategies to meet those needs:

    a. Express my need for balance and ask my brother if he is willing to take my mother to her next two doctor's appointments.

    b. Express my need for reliability and explore with my brother how I can increase my trust in counting on him for follow-through.

    c. Address my need for connection by finding something special I can offer to do with my ex-girlfriend that doesn't cost money.

4. Marshall quotes Gandhi's words at the head of this chapter: *"Let us become the change we seek in the world."* Give specific observations of how you are becoming the change you seek in the world.

Nine—Leader's Guide

Consider giving all participants who worked with the Individual Practice part of this week's assignment an opportunity to share their flow-charts (for Item #1) and "have to/choose to" lists (for Item #2). Ask participants to describe what was learned from each of the two processes they practiced. If necessary, split into two or three groups for part of today's session in order to create adequate time for everyone to share.

If participants did not do #1 of the Individual Practice at home, ask for someone who would enjoy demonstrating a "live practice" by volunteering something they did that they now regret. Support them through the process by offering cues at each step. Encourage them to verbalize whatever self-judgments or other thoughts come up for them as they proceed. Be sure to take time, remembering that the process is not simply to *identify* and *name* feelings and needs but to deeply *connect* with the aliveness inside themselves in this very moment.

If there is extra time after completing #1 and #2 of this week's Individual Practice, explore the subject of money as strategy and its underlying needs. You might end the session with having participants celebrate ways in which they are becoming the change they seek in the world (Item #4 of the Individual Practice).

NOTE: The following activity is offered for groups wanting further work on self-judging.

Internal Dialogue: Self, Self-judge, Self-defender

The awareness of our self-judgmental thoughts provides an opportunity for translation that leads to connection with our feelings and needs. If, however, when self-judgments start to arise, we are quick to censor them, to respond defensively, or to console ourselves, we add a further layer of thoughts blocking ourselves from our original feelings and needs. The following internal dialogue illustrates this effect.

Example of self-dialogue:

Self: *Hmm, what's this at the bottom of the bin? Oh, a whole stack of papers I'd forgotten about.*

Self-judge: *Aargh, look at all these overdue bills! I really messed up! Why can't I ever get myself together? It's not like it's all that hard to pay a few bills on time!*

Self-defender: *Let's not be so hard on ourselves. Everyone forgets sometimes.*

Self-judge: *Yeah, but I'm <u>always</u> forgetting things and <u>always</u> letting things slide and then of course I just have to pay for it later. I just can't believe how I'm always so . . .*

Self-defender: *Stop! You're <u>not</u> always this or that! Stop putting yourself down. Remember in NVC how we're not supposed to judge ourselves? It only makes things worse. Remember we're always doing the best we can and we're fine just as we are. So we made a little mistake and forgot something. Let's not make such a big deal of it! All we have to do is now is to sit down and pay the bills. We're gonna be okay.*

NOTE: This internal dialogue ends as the person sits down to pay bills.

Translating Self-dialogue

The following instructions refer to the sample self-dialogue given above. After you familiarize yourself with the suggested procedures, however, you may apply them to similar internal dialogues that participants volunteer.

1. Three participants sitting next to each other take the roles of the three voices (Self, Self-judge and Self-defender) by reading their respective lines.

2. Another participant empathizes with the Self-defender, reflecting back its feelings and needs. Take time: there may be several

layers of feelings and needs behind the voice that wants to console, defend, deny, or fix.

a. Self-defender: *Let's not be so hard on ourselves. Everyone forgets sometimes.*

   Empathize with the above voice: (Reflect back feelings and needs.)

b. Self-defender: *Stop! You're not always this or that! Stop putting yourself down. Remember in NVC how we're not supposed to judge ourselves? It only makes things worse. Remember we're always doing the best we can and we're fine just as we are. So we made a little mistake and forgot something. Let's not make such a big deal of it! All we have to do is now is to sit down and pay the bills. We're gonna be okay.*

   Empathize with the above voice:

3. After the feelings and needs of the Self-defender have been fully heard, the Self-defender will then be ready to empathize with the Self-judge. The Self-defender now helps the Self-judge connect with the feelings and needs beneath its judgments. (This is the "mourning" process.)

   a. Self-judge: *Aargh, look at all these overdue bills! I really messed up! Why can't I ever get myself together? It's not like it's all that hard to pay a few bills on time!*

   Empathize with the above voice:

   b. Self-judge: *Yeah, but I'm <u>always</u> forgetting things and always letting things slide and then of course I just have to pay for it later. I just can't believe how I'm always so . . .*

   Empathize with the above voice:

4. After the self-judgments have been fully translated into feelings and needs, the Self-judge will be ready to empathize with the Self.

    The Self-judge helps the Self to connect with the feelings and needs behind the choices that were made that resulted in the bills being overdue. (This is self-forgiveness.)

    Allow the Self to connect with the need(s) behind the choices that led to the bills being overdue:

5. Before ending, ask each participant to what degree they experienced a shift after having been empathically connected with. Invite others in the group to share what they observed and learned.

◎ Do you recall a moment when you cut short your own self-judgments?

a. Write down what that sounded like.

b. Now empathize with that voice.

Nine—Sample Responses to Leader's Guide

Responses for Internal Dialogue: Self, Self-judge, Self-defender

2a. Self-defender: Let's not be so hard on ourselves. Everyone forgets sometimes.

Empathy for self-defender: Are you anxious when you start hearing self-judgments because you so value compassion towards ourselves? Do you want to know that we can forgive ourselves for times when we've made mistakes?

2b. Self-defender: Stop! You're not always this or that! Stop putting yourself down. Remember in NVC how we're not supposed to judge ourselves? It only makes things worse. Remember we're always doing the best we can and we're fine just as we are. So we made a little mistake and forgot something. Let's not make such a big deal of it! All we have to do is now is to sit down and pay the bills. We're gonna be okay.

Empathy for self-defender: Do you feel distressed and want to trust that we will still accept ourselves, and be kind and understanding towards ourselves, even if we're discouraged with the choices we've made? And I wonder: Are you also feeling scared because you want to protect me from the pain and shame of hearing those judgments?

3a. Self-judge: Aargh, look at all these overdue bills! I really messed up! Why can't I ever get myself together? It's not like it's all that hard to pay a few bills on time!

Empathy for self-judge: Are you disappointed because you'd like to be able to count on yourself to get to tasks on time?

3b. Self-judge: Yeah, but I'm <u>always</u> forgetting things and always letting things slide and then of course I just have to pay for it later. I just can't believe how I'm always so . . .

Empathy for self-judge: It sounds like you feel really discouraged when you recall that this has happened more than once because you'd like to trust that you can learn from past mistakes? And are you also worried when you think of possible consequences because you value effective use of your time and money?

4. Allow the Self to connect with the need(s) behind the choices that led to the bills being overdue:

I can see I have been putting most of my attention outside of work this month into gardening, family and friends, and the new diet-and-exercise program. I made choices to use my time and energy in this way because I value good health, being with people I love and contributing to their well-being, connecting with the earth and nurturing new life on the planet.

◎ Review these sample responses, noticing how they are similar to or different from your own. What do you notice about these differences? How might you modify your own responses after reviewing these?

Exercises for the Chapter: Expressing Anger Fully

10

Ten—Individual Assignments

Reading Review

1. The author assures readers who are angry with social and political injustices that Nonviolent Communication does not regard anger as

   _____.

2. Of the four options for hearing a difficult message, which one are we choosing when we get angry?

3. What is the stimulus of anger?

4. Why is it so important to distinguish between stimulus and cause?

5. It serves to confuse stimulus and cause if you want to use _____ to control other people's behavior.

6. When we see someone doing something we think is hurtful, such as polluting the environment, the author suggests we are better off paying attention to_____ rather than_____.

7. In what way can anger be of use to us?

8. The author recommends that we repeatedly practice replacing the phrase, "I am angry because they . . ." with the phrase, _____.

9. What did the author learn from being punched in the face on two successive days?

10. What happens to our anger in the moment that we truly get in touch with our needs?

11. Why does the author emphasize the distinction between cause and stimulus on "practical and tactical" as well as philosophical grounds?

12. Violence results when people trick themselves into believing that _____.

13. Most people we talk to would be unable to focus on our needs when we express our needs to them by _____.

14. What happens when we get people to meet our current needs by shaming, guilt-tripping, or intimidating them?

15. Describe the four steps to expressing anger.

16. What might you need to do between Steps 3 and 4? Why?

17. What does the author suggest doing when violent thoughts arise in our heads?

18. Marshall did not want the man in the taxi to hear blame or to admit fault for being racist. Why?

19. Why might it be awkward for most of us just learning NVC to apply this process?

20. Explain the difference between expressing anger "superficially" and "fully."

Individual Practice

NOTE: Exercise #1 is to be completed in one sitting, and may take some time. Before beginning, read over the complete set of instructions as well as the next page, *What is Anger?*

---

1. Recall a time when you felt angry. Recapture the scenario by bringing to mind the details of that moment (what the place looked and

felt like, your physical posture, how the other person appeared to you, the sounds around you, etc.).

a. Identify the stimulus (or stimuli) of your anger in the form of observation(s).

b. What were the "should-thoughts" in your head?

c. Translate your "should-thinking" into needs. There may be several, so be sure to notice them all and to include, of course, all 4-D thoughts even if the word "should" itself is not present. (The 4-Ds of disconnection are Diagnosis, Denial of responsibility, Demand, and Deserve-oriented language—see Assignment Two.)

d. Allowing yourself ample time, sit quietly with the awareness of your unmet needs in that situation. "When I realize the deep need I had for _____ (and _____ and _____) and I realize these needs were not being fulfilled, I feel _____." Now go inside yourself and see what you find.

You might notice various physical sensations, emotions, and mind states (see the page, *What is Anger?*). Just fully be with whatever comes up, without needing to find "the right word" to express it.

In addition you will probably notice many kinds of thoughts and images coming and going—everything from "She certainly left a deep wound in me," to "This exercise is stupid," to "I'm never going to do that kind of thing again," etc. As a thought arises, simply recognize it as "Here's a thought." Then let it go, and gently bring your attention back to the feeling level, paying attention to physical sensations, emotions and mind states you are discovering in yourself.

If your mind wanders, bring it back to focus by repeating, "When I realize my needs for _____ are not being met, I feel _____ " Allow yourself to fully be with whatever feelings come up for you in the presence of this awareness of your unmet needs.

End this part without hurrying when you sense you are finished with the exploration.

What is Anger?

Anger is an experience of a constantly changing constellation of:

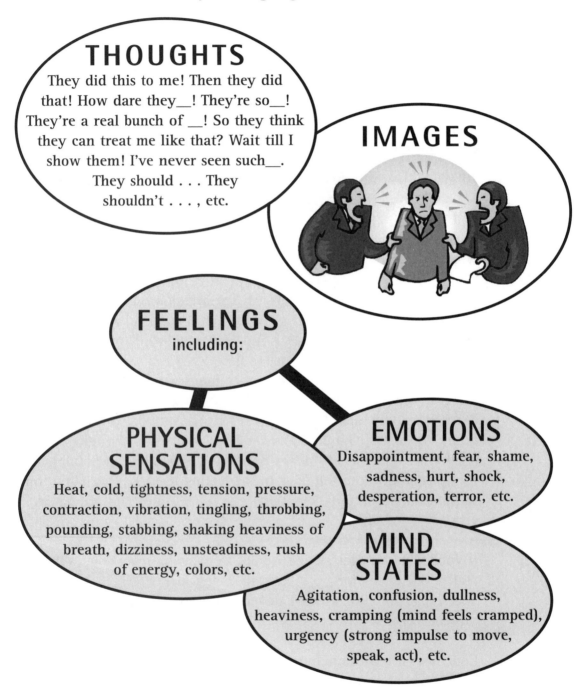

THOUGHTS

They did this to me! Then they did that! How dare they__! They're so__! They're a real bunch of __! So they think they can treat me like that? Wait till I show them! I've never seen such__. They should . . . They shouldn't . . . , etc.

IMAGES

FEELINGS
including:

PHYSICAL SENSATIONS

Heat, cold, tightness, tension, pressure, contraction, vibration, tingling, throbbing, pounding, stabbing, shaking heaviness of breath, dizziness, unsteadiness, rush of energy, colors, etc.

EMOTIONS
Disappointment, fear, shame, sadness, hurt, shock, desperation, terror, etc.

MIND STATES
Agitation, confusion, dullness, heaviness, cramping (mind feels cramped), urgency (strong impulse to move, speak, act), etc.

e. Now verbally identify the feelings (emotions) associated with your unmet needs in that situation.

f. Using the four components of the NVC process, "express your anger fully" as if you were addressing the other party in the present moment:

—observations (stimuli)

—feelings (underneath the anger)

—needs

—requests

g. Do you think the other party would be able to fully hear your feelings and needs as you expressed them in f. (above)? If not, write how you might express empathy for what they might be feeling and needing.

h. Use the 4 components of NVC to express yourself in this current moment:

"Having completed this exercise on anger,

"I feel _____

"because I _____

"and I would like_____ (this may be a request to yourself)."

i. What part of this process was easy or difficult for you? Why?

2. Divide a sheet of paper into two columns. On one column, list the judgments about other people that float most frequently in your head, using the cue "I don't like people who are . . ." For each judgment, ask yourself, "When I make that judgment of a person, what am I needing and not getting?" Write the need in the other column.

3. The next time you find yourself feeling anger, refer to the table in *Appendix 4, SSTOP Being Sabotaged by Anger!* Experiment following through with the process, watching your own thoughts and feelings

carefully, and jotting down in the columns what you observe and what you find in your heart and mind.

Ten—Leader's Guide

For most of us, the complete process of "expressing anger fully" often requires time. It is not a process of venting through the verbal use of the 4 components of NVC. It's not recommended that members take this session as an opportunity to direct angry feelings at each other with the expectation that they can pass through all the steps on the spot to arrive at a transformed heart space, although this certainly can happen. Instead, try introducing more extended "empathy sessions" in today's circle for anyone experiencing anger so that they may be fully heard and then supported through the "expressing anger fully" process. In addition to "empathy sessions," have participants share responses to Individual Practice items. You might use *Appendix 4 SSTOP! Being Sabotaged By Anger* to chart the process. The following activity is offered for additional practice in identifying "should-thoughts" and translating them to needs.

Activity 1: Identifying "Should-thinking"

Here is a list of angry thoughts and images. For each one determine:

    a. What are some associated "should-thoughts"?

    b. What are the unfulfilled need(s) behind them?

        1. "Teachers have no right to boss us around."

        2. "Barbara's a real slacker. She's had more time then anyone else to get her part of this project completed. Now we all have to pay."

        3. "Don't you dare raise your voice when you're talking to me!"

        4. "What the hell makes them think they're so much better than the rest of us?"

        5. "Nike, Starbucks, and all those fat-cat multi-nationals deserve to get their windows busted!"

6. "I can't stand the way she talks so sweet, as if she really gives a damn about any one of us."

7. "You pervert!"

8. "I can't believe he is charging me for the ride! How many millions of times have I given him and his brothers free rides when they were kids!!"

9. "You're so insensitive—didn't you even notice that I was limping throughout the whole evening?"

10. "Idiot!"

⊚ Try this on your own. Record your responses in your notebook.

Ten—Sample Responses to Leader's Guide

Responses for Activity 1: Identifying "Should-thinking"

Identifying "should-thinking" and possible needs behind "should-thoughts."

1. Should-thinking: *Teachers shouldn't boss us around. Teachers should treat us differently.* Needs: autonomy, understanding

2. Should-thinking: *Barbara should do her part. She shouldn't make us all suffer.* Needs: consideration, reliability

3. Should-thinking: *You shouldn't raise your voice when you talk to me. You should talk nicely.* Needs: respect, safety

4. Should-thinking: *They shouldn't be so stuck-up. They should know better.* Needs: understanding, respect

5. Should-thinking: *They should suffer because they cause others to suffer. They shouldn't get rich by exploiting people.* Needs: mutuality (the need for balance, equal give and take), compassion

6. Should-thinking: *She should be real. She shouldn't be such a hypocrite.* Needs: authenticity, trust

7. Should-thinking: *You shouldn't think or do that. You should behave responsibly.* Needs: safety, respect

8. Should-thinking: *He shouldn't charge me. He should remember how often I gave him a ride.* Needs: support, mutuality

9. Should-thinking: *You should have noticed I was limping. You shouldn't be so insensitive.* Needs: awareness, visibility

10. Should-thinking: *You should know better. You shouldn't say such stupid things.* Needs: consideration, understanding

Review these sample responses, noticing how they are similar to or different from your own. What do you notice about these differences? How might you modify your own responses after reviewing these?

Exercises for the Chapter: The Protective Use of Force

Eleven—Individual Assignments

Reading Review

1. Under what circumstances might we choose to use force?

2. Identify the differences between the protective use of force and the punitive use of force in terms of:

    a. intentions behind the use of force

    b. assumptions about why human beings make mistakes and how correction takes place

3. What particular concern does the author emphasize regarding the use of corporal punishment on children?

4. What other forms of punishment are mentioned in addition to physical punishment?

5. What are likely negative consequences when we use punishment as a way to motivate people to change their behavior?

6. Instead of punishing them, what does the author suggest doing with children who are hurting others?

7. What two questions might we ask ourselves first when we threaten to punish someone in order to get them to do what we want?

8. What are some common motivating forces behind children cleaning their rooms? What are some values that parents often want their children to be responding to when those children clean their rooms?

9. What is the level of moral development that NVC fosters?

10. To what does the author attribute the success of the "do nothing room"?

Individual Practice

1. Can you recall an incident where you used "protective" force? What elements were present that led you to define your use of force as "protective" in this situation? Can you imagine a similar situation where the use of force would have qualified as "punitive?" If so, what differences do you notice between the two situations?

2. Can you recall doing something that caused harm and that you now regret?

   a. What do you think caused you to do what you did?

   b. Is your behavior due to your being bad (due to human evil, including weakness of will)? Is it due to ignorance (including lack of skill to live out values and intentions)? Or is it something else?

   c. If you believe that you (as well as other humans) behave out of "badness," how would you correct such "badness"?

   d. If you believe that people behave out of "ignorance," what kind of correctional process would you recommend?

3. How might you appeal to the nation's correctional system to switch from the punitive to the protective use of force? For those who are incarcerated: are you able to base your appeal on your own experiences?

4. For those in parenting roles: Write down five things you would like your children to do (or do more often). Next to each item write down what you want their reason(s) to be for doing it.

5. The following exercise leads you through the process of "mourning in NVC," and is an extension of your practice in Assignment Nine. It addresses how we can face our mistakes and grow beyond them in a way that is not oriented towards punishment (including the punishment of ourselves through guilt and shame).

   a. When you recall having caused harm in the incident mentioned earlier (#2, above), what do you say to yourself about what you did?

b. Check to see if you were speaking to yourself in NVC in a. above. If not, translate what you wrote using the four components:

  - *When I recall* (your observation of what you did) _____

  - *I feel* _____

  - *because I need* (or value) (or: *it doesn't meet my need for*) _____

  - *and I would like to request of myself* _____.

EXAMPLE:

  - When I recall telling my little son, *"You have to go to school, like it or not!"*

  - I feel anguish

  - because I value understanding and support.

  - My request of myself is to write down the words I would have liked to have said to him, and put them on my bathroom mirror to help me remember how to empathize next time.

c. Now return to the moment when you took the action that you now regret. Recall the circumstances of that moment—both external (what was going on out there) and internal (what was going on inside of yourself). Empathize with the person who you were (who took the action you now regret):

  - When I (saw, heard, recalled . . .) _____

  - I felt _____

  - because I needed_____

  - The strategy I chose to meet my needs (above) was to _____ (the action you now regret).

EXAMPLE:

  - When I heard my son say, *"Mom, I am not going to school*

tomorrow, or ever again!"

- I felt scared and desperate

- because I value education and self-reliance (I needed to know that he was getting the skills that would allow him to live an independent, productive life).

- The strategy I chose to meet my needs (above) was to say, *"You have to go to school, like it or not!"*

Eleven—Leader's Guide

This chapter may stimulate questions regarding theories of human behavior and their social applications and consequences. As the leader, focus and also limit such discussions by defining the specific questions being raised and allotting a limited time. If disagreements begin to heat up, use the opportunity to encourage the practice of listening, reflecting, and slowing down.

Continue with the practice activities your circle has been developing over the last months. If you have not yet incorporated role-playing in your repertoire, you may want to introduce this after reviewing *Suggestions for Role-Play* in this workbook.

Activity 1: Schoolyard Episode

The following episode involving blame and punishment in an institutional setting is offered for your group's consideration.

Schoolyard

1. Something happens.

2. Something else happens.

3. Something else happens.

4. A Jamaican child says, "You white honky" to a white child.

5. The white child says, "You nigger" to the Jamaican child.

6. Jamaican child goes to the teacher and says, "He called me nigger."

7. Teacher tells white child, "We don't tolerate racism at our school. Go to the principal's office for the rest of the day."

Next morning

8. White child's parents call the principal, *"Here's what happened to our child. We want an apology from the teacher and the*

school for this outrageous reverse racism."

Write a separate line of empathy for each of the following people:

a. the Jamaican child

b. the white child when hearing the words of the Jamaican child

c. the teacher

d. the white child when being sent to principal's office

e. the white child's parents

f. the principal

Now imagine that each person had received the line of empathy you wrote from the person listed below them. How do you think this chain of events might have been different?

◎ Try this on your own.

Eleven—Sample Responses to Leader's Guide

Responses for Activity 1: Schoolyard Episode

NOTE: The sample lines of empathy below express only feelings and needs. There are no requests. Requests will surface only after the person has received adequate empathy (through a series of empathic interactions) and is ready to address solutions to the situation.

---

1. (to Jamaican child:) *Do you feel frustrated because you would like everyone to be included in the game?*

2. (to white child:) *Are you upset because you need more respect?*

3. (to teacher:) *Are you concerned because you want to see respect for all races being taught and modeled at this school?* (Universal need here is for respect.)

4. (to white child:) *Do you feel annoyed because you would like to be understood for what happened?*

5. (to white child's parents:) *Do you feel dismayed and disturbed because you value integrity and want to see equal respect accorded to all races?*

6. (to principal:) *Do you feel stressed and do you need some reassurance that this can be resolved harmoniously, through mutual understanding?* (Universal needs here are for understanding and harmony.)

Review these sample responses, noticing how they are similar to or different from your own. What do you notice about these differences? How might you modify your own responses after reviewing these?

Exercises for the Chapter: Liberating Ourselves and Counseling Others

Twelve—Individual Assignments

Reading Review

1. Growing up as children, as well as in our adult lives, we have all received messages of ways in which we are limited or "don't measure up." Yet, we are often unconscious of these messages and of the pain they engender. Why?

2. What historical reason does Marshall give for our lack of literacy regarding needs?

3. Give examples of cultural training that keeps us from knowing our own needs.

4. How can we liberate ourselves from the limitations and pain generated by our cultural conditioning?

5. According to Marshall, depression occurs because we are disconnected from _____.

6. What does Marshall suggest that we focus on when we are faced with a challenging or stressful situation?

7. How did Marshall free himself from anger-provoking messages while driving on the freeway?

8. Why was Martin Buber skeptical that someone in the role of a psychotherapist could actually do psychotherapy?

9. When counseling distressed people, instead of trying to figure out what is wrong with them, what questions would Marshall ask himself instead?

Individual Practice

NOTE: A week's time is needed for the exercise described in #1.

---

1. This exercise asks you to observe yourself over the duration of a week. In your mind's eye, go over a typical week and notice where the high-stress moments are, e.g. getting out of bed, driving in traffic, children fighting, presenting a lecture, meeting with the boss, calling your mother, etc.

   Over the course of the week, pay special attention to what you think and say to yourself during these moments. If possible, jot down the actual words that come up in your head during the situation.

   a. Later in the day or week, review what you observed of your thoughts and inner dialogues. Were there judgments of yourself, the situation, or other people? Did your thoughts embody other forms of life-alienating communication? Translate them into feelings and needs.

   b. Ask yourself, "What do I truly want to see happen in this situation?"

   c. Then ask, "What specifically can I do to contribute to the changes I want to see happen?"

2. "We've all learned things that limit us as human beings, whether from well-intentioned parents, teachers, clergy, or others." What did you learn as a child about yourself that had (or still has) the effect of limiting you as a human being?

3. "It takes tremendous energy and awareness to recognize . . . destructive learning and to transform it into thoughts and behaviors which are of value and of service to life." If you are interested in making this transformation, what are you doing or what might you do to invite "tremendous energy" or "tremendous awareness" into your life?

4. Take an internal conflict, preferably one that is current for you:

   a. Write down what the conflicting voices are saying.

   b. Translate the dialogue using all four NVC components for each voice.

      (See example of dialogue between "career woman" and "responsible mother" under Resolving Internal Conflicts subheading of this chapter in the book.)

5. What kind of "inner environment" do you wish to experience? What can you do to generate it?

Twelve—Leader's Guide

For today's circle emphasize the theme of internal talk. Encourage members of the group during this time together to be especially alert to the words inside their own heads. It may be helpful for each person to have pen and paper in hand, jotting down pieces of internal talk that appear during the meeting. Provide pauses in between activities, inviting those who are willing to share what they have recorded. Support the translation of life-alienated internal talk into NVC.

Invite the group to select activities for today's session. Besides any regular practices you have found helpful, consider:

- sharing responses to Individual Practice, #1 and #4.

- Activity 1 (below, requires 1 hour)—Role-play responding to people in distress

- Activity 2 (below, about 20 minutes)—Translating self-dialogue

If there is interest in psychotherapy and in reviewing other questions in Individual Practice, the group might like to set a time for such discussions to ensure adequate opportunity for actual practice.

Activity 1: Responding to People in Distress

Role-play practice: Responding in NVC to people in distress who approach us with hope for relief (regarding problems that are unrelated to us personally).

1. Choose partners to work in pairs.

2. If numbers are uneven, one person may serve as time-keeper and observer. Switch time-keepers at Step 8, below.

3. Decide who is Partner A and who is Partner B.

4. Time-keeper invites one minute of silence, during which time:

5. Partner A, bring to mind a current situation of distress for which you are seeking relief.

6. Partner B, center yourself in NVC consciousness, cultivating receptivity to hearing:

   a. What is this person feeling?

   b. What do they need?

   c. How do I feel in response to this person, and what needs of mine are behind my feelings?

   d. What action or decision would I request this person to take in the belief that it would enable them to live more happily?

7. In the 20 minutes partners have to interact in this segment of the activity, the pair may either play themselves (as friends, NVC practitioners, etc.), or choose a role for Partner B that he or she can comfortably assume, e.g. neighborhood watch captain, legal aide, child's teacher, elected official, nurse, counselor, etc. (Be aware how much time you spend choosing this role!)

8. Time-keeper: indicate when 20 minutes are up. Then give 10 minutes for each pair to complete their role-play and debrief what they observed and learned.

   Switch time-keepers. Partners A and B reverse roles, repeating Steps 5-8, above.

◎ Try Activity 1 on your own as an internal dialogue playing both roles. Record your internal dialogue in your notebook.

Activity 2: Translating Self-dialogue

1. One person reads the following self-dialogue out loud, *slowly* and *with expression.*

2. Others be listening for feelings and needs underneath the words.

3. Going around the room, each participant takes the opportunity to translate a line.

4. After all feedback has been heard and discussed, one person will read the original self-dialogue in its entirety out loud once again, while

5. A second participant follows with an NVC translation that reflects the group's understanding and learning.

It's disgusting the way I stuffed my mouth at that party. I am so weak-willed, I just don't have the slightest self-discipline. Nobody else was eating the way I was. If I keep behaving this way, I'll have to walk sideways to get through doors! People will really think I'm gross. Well, what right do they have to judge me; they should mind their own business . . . Anyway, I shouldn't be concerned about how people look at me. I deserve to enjoy what I enjoy. What's wrong with that? . . . . Oh, come on, don't be stupid, stop kidding yourself. You know what's wrong with stuffing your face . . .

> ◎ Try Activity 2 on your own. Translate the negative internal dialogue into NVC.

Twelve—Sample Response to Leader's Guide

Responses for Activity 2: Translating Self-dialogue

I feel disappointed with the amount of food I ate at the party. I want to be able to trust myself when it comes to eating the amount of food I really want to eat. I am worried because I want to cultivate a physical appearance that I think is attractive to others—I want to be accepted. But even more, I want to be able to accept myself—whether or not others do. I am determined to make choices that serve my life, that bring me happiness, rather than make choices to accommodate other people's judgments of me. I have a need to accept myself for making choices that bring me happiness. I want to celebrate my enjoyment, fully relish the joy of my taste buds with each morsel I receive . . . mmm . . . I also want to support my choice to maintain my current figure, to eat in a way where I take joy in the consequences. So, what can I do here to ensure my happiness around these two needs?

 Review this sample response and compare it with your own. What do you notice about the differences?

Exercises for the Chapter: Expressing Appreciation in NVC

Thirteen—Individual Assignments

Reading Review

1. In what ways do praise and compliments qualify as forms of "life-alienating" communication?

2. What do managers and teachers mean when they say "it works" in regard to praise and compliments? What reservation does Marshall express regarding this claim?

3. Why is Marshall concerned about the use of positive feedback as a means to influence other people's behavior?

4. What is the purpose of using NVC to express appreciation?

5. Which three components are present when we express appreciation in NVC?

6. Why do many of us have difficulty receiving appreciation gracefully?

7. When receiving appreciation, what attitude might we take to help us steer clear of both smugness and false humility?

8. What kinds of resistance did Marshall notice in himself regarding the expression of appreciation towards his Uncle Julius?

Individual Practice

Cultivating Gratitude

In the book, *Being Peace*, Vietnamese poet and Zen master Thich Nhat Hanh writes, *If you are a poet, you will see clearly that there is a cloud floating in this sheet of paper. Without a cloud there will be no water; without water, the trees cannot grow; and without trees, you cannot make paper . . . And if you look more deeply . . . you see not only the cloud and the sunshine in it, but that everything is here: the wheat that became the bread for the logger to eat, the logger's father—everything is in this sheet of paper.*

As our understanding of interconnectedness transforms into living reality, joy and gratitude spring forth in our every encounter with life. NVC consciousness deepens our connection with our own life energy and what we value at each moment, increasingly allowing us to see the way our lives and our universally shared needs are being supported from so many directions.

1. Choose a meal when you are able to take some time to contemplate the food.

   * What do you see in your plate?

   * What elements?

   * Whose lives or sacrifice of lives?

   * Whose hands, hearts, sweat, dreams, etc.?

We develop this sense of interconnectedness by acknowledging all that is eaten in its original form—envisioning the wheat that comprises the bread, the milk of the cow, the pod of the pea. The ocean of the fish. And the sun that feeds them all. We take in the sacred, the germ of life, like the Eucharist, in gratitude and respect. —Stephen Levine

---

NOTE: Individual Practice #2 is a month-long practice

---

2. Over the course of a month, ask yourself on a daily basis, *What happened*

in the last 24 hours for which I am thankful? This does not need to take more than a few minutes, but try doing it consistently—either before or after a regular activity in your life (e.g. getting out of bed, commuting, lunch, evening news, etc.).

3. Think of someone in your life who did (or is doing) something you appreciate. Send them an NVC appreciation: it can be a brief note or a long letter.

   When you send it, be aware if you are expecting anything in return. (If you want something back, you might make a clear request, remembering to include the feelings and needs behind your request.)

4. "What appreciation might someone give you that would leave you jumping for joy?"

5. In your everyday interactions, practice translating praises and compliments into observations, feelings, and needs. In the beginning, when receiving a compliment, you may want to do this translation internally. After some practice you may become confident that your translation will be heard as joint celebration rather than as correction or self-aggrandizement.

EXAMPLE:

   a. Internal (to yourself)—after having just made a delivery to a customer: *He just said 'Great job' to me. He must be happy. He's happy because I . . . wait, what's the need? Okay, he's happy because he sees that the furniture all arrived intact and on time. His needs for safety and reliability have been fulfilled.*

   b. External (interaction with other)
   Customer: *Hey, great job!*
   You: *Thanks, you like being able to rely on deliveries arriving safely and on time?*

   After hearing the customer's needs that were met through your words or action, ask yourself, "What am I feeling now? And why?" This is self-appreciation: "I feel buoyant because I met my own needs for contributing to life and for integrity—doing what I said I would."

Thirteen—Leader's Guide

Provide lots of space for the joy of appreciation in this session that concludes the book and curriculum. Try weaving the theme of appreciation into the Remembrance, check-ins, and closing circle.

Activity 1: Role-play

a. Take 5 minutes to silently bring to mind someone in your life whom you appreciate: Recall what they did, how you felt when they did it, and what need of yours was met. (It is not necessary for the person you choose to still be living.)

b. Choose someone to role-play that person and fully express your appreciation in NVC out loud to them.

c. Listener role: receive the appreciation with empathy. After taking it in fully, express any feelings that arise in you and where they come from (i.e. the needs behind them).

> ◎ Try completing a. and b. on your own.

Activity 2: Appreciate someone in the circle.

This can be interspersed throughout the meeting. Agree to use a particular gesture and a phrase like, "I have an appreciation" to "interrupt" the session at any time in order to express appreciation for something someone just did or said.

> ◎ Try expressing appreciation in this manner to a friend, family member, or co-worker.

(Leader: be sure to congratulate yourself and your group if you get nowhere with today's agenda of activities because the whole session got taken up by such interruptions.)

Activity 3: Sharing Individual Practice

For each of the five items listed in Individual Practice, see if there is at least one person in the circle willing to share what they've learned.

If not very many people did #4 at home, take time in the circle to do this. (*"What appreciation might someone give you that would leave you jumping for joy?"*)

Activity 4: Self-appreciation

Leader, give the following instructions to the group:

What do you appreciate about yourself and why? If it is a quality in yourself you appreciate, are you able to recall something specific you did or said that illustrates that quality?

What values or needs of yours are met by the behavior or quality you've identified?

As you recognize this aspect of yourself that you appreciate, what feelings do you notice?

Allow 5 minutes of silence, and then go around in a circle for each person to express their self-appreciation. Suggest that the group takes two breaths together after each person's sharing and to reserve any comments until the round has been completed.

At the end, ask for feedback on the experience of appreciating oneself, expressing it to others, and hearing others appreciate themselves. Encourage feedback-givers to stay connected to needs and feelings rather than to analyze their experience:

Habitual expression: *Given that I don't generally toot my own horn in public like this, it felt really kind of weird at first, but then I figured it was okay because everyone was doing it . . .*

NVC expression: *At first I felt a little bit, uh, embarrassed. I was nervous, I guess maybe needing acceptance, understanding.*

Then when I realized we were all doing it, I kind of relaxed, and figured I could trust us to accept each other—that I won't be judged for being arrogant or something.

◎   Try this on your own. Record your responses in your notebook.

Activity 5: Cultivating gratitude

A daily practice of gratitude can radically change our lives. The only resource it requires is a few minutes a day, but establishing any new habit takes commitment. We are fortunate to have a practice circle where we can give and receive support around this intention.

Leader: Review instructions for Individual Practice, item #2. Ask if anyone wants to commit to experimenting with this practice, and if so, how might the rest of us support them. It may be helpful for individuals to think of specific times and places they will do this practice, to share this information with the group, and to hear how others are approaching it. Over the course of the next month, be sure to allot time at each meeting to share individual progress (or lack of it) around this piece.

Thirteen—Sample Responses to Leader's Guide

Responses for Activity 4: Self-appreciation

1. What do you appreciate about yourself and why?

   "I appreciate myself when I see myself acting upon an intention. I appreciate this quality because I value effectiveness: bringing dreams to fruition."

2. If it is a quality in yourself you appreciate, are you able to recall something specific you did or said that illustrates that quality?

   "A specific example might be what I am doing now—finishing writing this workbook."

3. What values or needs of yours are met by the behavior or quality you've identified?

   "This action meets not only my need for effectiveness, but also for contribution and support. I want to contribute to people learning NVC and especially to support those who are doing it on their own."

   "And it also meets my need for meaning and purposeful activity, creativity, challenge, and enjoyment. And growth and learning. Wow."

4. As you recognize this aspect of yourself that you appreciate, what feelings do you notice?

   "Sitting here with the appreciation for myself, I am aware of feelings of surprise, joy, feeling moved, something like awe . . . My eyes are drawn towards the window, to the mountains (hands still on the keyboard) . . . I feel my heart overflowing with gratitude, feeling affinity with the jagged white peaks and sensing that I am part of the same mystery."

   "I feel excited to be part of life, to recognize the gifts I have access to. I feel surprised that I am feeling all these feelings (I started the morning meaning to write a quick Sample Response to complete this part of the workbook)."

"I'm also noticing a hint of a humbling feeling: did I really think I could get away with mechanically going through the motions of an NVC practice—even one I made up a year ago myself?"

"And I am feeling such deep appreciation for Marshall and for NVC, for bringing me back over and over again to my connection with life."

5. How do you feel about having appreciated yourself and expressing it publicly? Any feedback on the process?

"I feel just a slight bit insecure, unsure . . . maybe vulnerable . . . needing to trust that there is understanding and acceptance for what I am sharing publicly."

"As to the process, I am amused that writing this Sample Response took two hours rather than 30 minutes, but I am glad because I value responses based on authentic experience."

◉ After reading the above sample, review the response you had recorded in your notebook for this activity. Look at the process you used to appreciate yourself and the sample above. What similarities or differences do you notice and what do you learn from noticing these?

APPENDICES

Appendix 1. Suggestions for Further Practice of NVC

1. Undertake a 13-Month Practice

Many who undertake one assignment per week recognize the potential for deeper learning if given the time to delve further into the materials offered. This is especially true if you're an individual working through the material on your own. If you wish to continue a more structured practice after the 13 weeks, consider taking the theme of each chapter and "living with it" for a month.

Thus, during the first month your intention would be, on a daily basis, to develop awareness of moments when you give from the heart and moments when you give from places other than the heart. Make a mental or written note for the purpose of revisiting the moment at a later time when you feel more confident you could do something other than say "yes" when you mean "I'd rather do something different." The challenge of revisiting the moment can be seen as an opportunity to deepen your NVC consciousness. Over time, you will celebrate how you are able to say "no" in such a way that others clearly hear the needs to which you are saying "yes."

During the second month, remind yourself each day to be alert for external and internal messages that contribute to disconnection from feelings and needs. Notice the times you hear or say any of the following words: *should, must, can't, have to, supposed to, ought to.* Be aware of moments when you use manipulation, coercion, and punishment (or reward) as a strategy for getting what you want, or when your real purpose behind engaging someone is to blame, shame or guilt-trip them. Stay awake to choices you make at home and at work that are motivated by extrinsic reward. Pay attention to the moments when you are giving or receiving compliments: "Oh, what a good job! I'm so proud of you." "You are a great son (mother, worker, student, lover, communicator)." Are you doing what you do in order to receive praise and win approval? Or are you celebrating a moment when you happily contributed to another's well-being, or happily received a gift from another?

During the third month, concentrate on separating your evaluations from observations. Continue in this way, focusing on the specific theme of each chapter for an entire month.

2. Reenact Unfulfilling or Confusing Encounters

Make it a practice to review any interaction with another person (or with yourself!) that in hindsight you wish you had handled differently. You might write down or record the dialogue as you recall it and identify places where you became disconnected. (For example, suppose you heard a parent talking to a child in a tone or volume you didn't enjoy. Your immediate reaction might have been to blame the parent for being so "uncaring" or the child for being such a "brat." Or it might be an instance from childhood when you heard someone in the family reciting what was wrong with you.) Use your NVC skills to translate either your own or the other person's lines. Recall what you felt and needed, as well as what you said and did that contributed to getting—or not getting—your needs met. When you find yourself blaming yourself for not having behaved in an "NVC way," be sure to do the practice below.

3. Practice Giving Yourself Empathy

Over and over again, whenever you find yourself in pain, stop to give yourself empathy. If you cannot do it on the spot, freeze-frame the moment and bring it back later to give yourself some belated empathy. As you become more adept at offering yourself "emergency first aid empathy" the habit deepens in you to respond immediately to any distress by getting in touch with your feelings and needs. For those occasions that seem particularly troubling or complex, take time to write out your internal dialogue. First, give free rein to the part of you that expresses itself through habitual language, thoughts, and images. Then take the role of an empathic listener and reflect back observations, feelings, needs, and requests for each of the statements in the dialogue.

4. Explore Other Materials

The Center for Nonviolent Communication is continually developing new materials to support the learning of NVC. An annotated list of printed materials, audiotapes, videotapes, and CDs is provided at the end of this workbook. Watching a videotape with a friend (or group of friends) can be a fun way to review NVC while building like-minded support for yourself.

Even though you are choosing to study NVC on your own, pairing up with an "NVC buddy" whom you can call upon for help, feedback, and empathy can be a very fulfilling part of your practice.

Appendix 2. Feelings Lists

Feelings likely to occur when our needs <u>are</u> being met

AFFECTIONATE
friendly
loving
open
openhearted
sympathetic
tender
warm
ALERT
centered
clearheaded
mindful
steady
AWED
amazed
astonished
bedazzled
enchanted
enthralled
entranced
inspired
spellbound
wonder
CONFIDENT
empowered
expectant
hopeful
optimistic

proud
relieved
safe
secure
CONTENT
blissful
cheerful
comfortable
easy
glad
happy
pleased
DELIGHTED
adventurous
amused
carefree
high
lighthearted
mirth
playful
pleasure
ENERGETIC
alive
buoyant
creative
eager
ebullient
fresh

healthy
invigorated
vigorous
vital
zestful
EXCITED
ardent
enthusiastic
fervent
passionate
FREE
INTERESTED
absorbed
aroused
curious
engrossed
fascinated
inquisitive
intrigued
stimulated
JUBILANT
ecstatic
elated
exhilarated
exuberant
exultant
joyful
joyous

rapturous
thrilled
PEACEFUL
attuned
calm
composed
equanimous
quiet
reverent
tranquil
RELAXED
dreamy
languid
mellow
rested
SATISFIED
fulfilled
sated
THANKFUL
appreciative
expansive
grateful
gratified
moved
touched

Feelings likely to occur when our needs <u>are</u> <u>not</u> being met

AGONY
anguish
bereaved
broken-hearted
distress
grief
hurt
miserable
misery
mournful
pain
sad
sorrow
woe
wretched

ANGRY
enraged
furious
indignant
ire
outraged
vengeful

ANNOYED
aggravated
aroused
displeased
exasperated
frustrated
impatient
irked

irritated
miffed
peeved
vexed

AVERSION
alienated
animosity
bitter
disgusted
dislike
hate
hostile
loathing
repugnance
repulsed
resentment

DISAPPOINTED
agitated
alarmed
discouraged
disgruntled
disheartened
dismayed
disquiet
dissatisfied
disturbed
perturbed
rattled
startled
surprised

troubled
turbulent
turmoil
uncomfortable
uneasy
unsettled
upset

DISCONNECTED
aloof
apathetic
cold
contemptuous
cool
distant
indifferent
inhibited
nonchalant
numb
passive
pity
reluctant
remote
removed
reserved
unconcerned
unmoved
withdrawn

EMBARRASSED
ashamed
deflated

guilty
insecure
regretful
remorseful
shy
sorry
unsure of self

ENVIOUS
desirous
longing
nostalgic
pining
wistful
yearning

FEARFUL
anxious
apprehensive
daunted
dread
edgy
foreboding
frightened
guarded
horror
insecure
jittery
leery
mistrustful
nervous
panicky

petrified

scared

suspicious

terror

unnerved

wary

worried

GLOOMY

dejected

depressed

despairing

despondent

forlorn

hopeless

lonely

melancholy

mopey

pessimistic

resigned

TENSE

burdened

burnt out

constricted

cranky

depleted

distracted

distraught

encumbered

exhausted

fidgety

fragile

frazzled

intense

irritable

listless

off-centered

overwhelmed

restless

sensitive

stressed

stretched

ungrounded

vulnerable

CONFUSED

ambivalent

befuddled

conflicted

discombobulated

dizzy

doubtful

dubious

hesitant

in a daze

indecisive

lost

mystified

perplexed

puzzled

tentative

torn

uncertain

unclear

unsure

TIRED

bored

draggy

enervated

fatigued

heavy

lethargic

lifeless

low life energy

sleepy

weary

Appendix 3. Universal Needs List

The core of NVC Consciousness: "What is the need here?"

At the core of NVC is the awareness of the life-energy that is stirring in us in this moment. We see this life-energy related to a quality we cherish that sustains life. It may be expressed as a particular dream, need, want, or desire whose fulfillment or lack of fulfillment causes our feelings.

In NVC, we try to identify the "universal needs" that are common to all human beings—qualities that sustain life that we all cherish. Besides essential requirements for physical survival, such as air, food, sleep, etc., all human beings across all cultures share some basic needs (e.g. connection, autonomy, purpose, safety, respect, etc.) in order to thrive or to lead fulfilling lives and realize their human potential. We clearly distinguish these basic needs from more specific wants and desires that generate the strategies (specific to time, place, persons, or actions) by which we fulfill basic needs. These strategies and solutions are expressed through "requests" rather than identified as "needs"—a crucial distinction in NVC.

The following list of needs is neither exhaustive nor definitive. While needs are universal, these words are simply words and different people may use different words to convey a perceived need. The expression of needs is not a science, but an art that we each cultivate for ourselves. As we develop our vocabulary of needs, our objective is not to achieve correctness, but to deepen awareness.

Universal Needs

Interdependent Needs

To receive as well as to extend to others:

acceptance, inclusion

appreciation

(confirmation that a positive
contribution has been made)

compassion

(caring response to a perceived pain)

connection

consideration

(of our and others' needs or preferences)

cooperation

community

(being part of something larger
than ourselves)

empathy

honesty

(honest feedback on our words and
behaviors that enables us to learn from
past behaviors and limitations)

warmth, closeness, intimacy

respect, self-respect

support, nurturance

trust, reassurance

understanding

(to understand and be understood)

visibility

(to see and be seen or noticed)

Safety and health

security

dependability, consistency

Harmony and balance

beauty, order, peace

wholeness, equality, mutuality

inspiration, communion

Autonomy and authenticity

autonomy

(to choose one's goals, values, dreams
and ways to realize them)

integrity

(to live one's values)

authenticity

(to be true to oneself)

Clarity and awareness

consciousness

understanding

(the need for knowledge,
wisdom, experience)

Purpose and effectiveness

contribution

(to the enrichment of life)

meaning

purposeful activity, work

growth

competence

creativity, self-expression

Rest and play

enjoyment

challenge, stimulation,

ease, relaxation

celebration and mourning

(of life and the cycles of birth, death)

Appendix 4. SSTOP! Being Sabotaged by Anger

S	S	T	O	P
STIMULUS **What someone says** (their actual words): "Hey, you idiot." **What someone does** (their action): He knocked your radio to the ground. **A particular situation, object, or scene:** coming home to find your mailbox damaged	**SHOULD–THINKING** Cause of anger	**TRANSLATE TO NEEDS** Universal human need(s)	**OPEN TO FEELINGS** Physical sensations Emotions underlying anger	**PRESENT REQUEST** Something concretely do-able that you can ask of yourself or another person to meet your present needs

Appendix 5. Individual Feedback Form

(Permission granted to photocopy as needed.)

NVC Practice Group
INDIVIDUAL FEEDBACK FORM

Name: _____

Date of session: _____

My observations, feelings, and needs (met and unmet) regarding

1. today's meeting: _____

_____

_____

_____

2. my participation: _____

_____

_____

_____

3. others' participation: _____

_____

_____

_____

4. the leader's facilitation: _____

_____

_____

_____

5. what I learned today: _____

_____

_____

_____

Appendix 6. Group Feedback Form

(Permission granted to photocopy as needed.)

NVC Practice Group
MONTHLY GROUP FEEDBACK FORM

Month/year: _____

Group: _____

The leader of the last meeting of each month will facilitate a discussion to solicit feedback from the group, and then fill out this form afterwards.

Reflecting upon our month of practice together, these are

1. some things we are pleased with: _____
   _____
   _____

2. some challenges and concerns we face: _____
   _____
   _____

3. some new ways of doing things we want to try next month: _____
   _____
   _____

4. some ways in which we do not all agree: _____
   _____
   _____

5. some things we have learned: _____
   _____
   _____
   _____
   _____

Appendix 7. NVC Process Tracking Chart

(Permission granted to photocopy as needed.)

NVC Process
TRACKING CHART

Use this chart to track your steps in the NVC dance.

	HONESTY	EMPATHY
OBSERVATION		
FEELING		
NEED		
REQUEST		*

*problem-solve only after having fully empathized with the other person's feelings and needs.

Appendix 8. Further Resources

A partial list of the many resources currently available from the Center for Nonviolent Communication is included at the end of this Workbook. The following are reviews of some of those resources by various NVC practitioners.

The Giraffe Classroom by Nancy Sokol Green

In her 121-page workbook, Ms. Green shares ideas from her 5th grade classroom, where she has, for example, a corner of the room set up with various props for a "Ten-minute Vacation" (for Hawaii, camping, etc.).

Green offers NVC facilitators in the classroom various teaching concepts, ways of evaluating, disciplining, etc. She focuses on cooperative learning, the use of humor, and on fitting to the students'—rather than the teacher's—needs. Learning is approached not as an objective but as an ongoing, open-ended experience. Expression of feelings and wants is encouraged by everyone in the classroom.

There are eleven activities that address feelings in the classroom; the use of music, poetry, collage and science is integrated into these activities to make them real and alive. Green uses well-known characters such as Dick Tracy, Humpty Dumpty, and Little Red Riding Hood to illustrate the use of life-alienating communication.

Before I reviewed this book, I thought I would only buy it if I were to actually work in a classroom. Now I see, however, that many of the concepts are relevant to beginner NVC learners of any age. If you are interested in sharing NVC with others, this book offers lots of fun ways to do it. (Reviewed by M. Vestan)

NVC: The Basics as I Know and Use Them by Wayland Myers, Ph.D.

This booklet provides a concise description and discussion of Nonviolent Communication that I find clear, easy to read, and handy to use as a quick reference for the main points of the NVC process. In addition, Myers presents to-the-point discussions of real life relationships and situations that offer challenges of how we use NVC. I very much enjoy his presentation of the purpose of the process as well as his organization of the process into sections about "how to share and listen," "what to share and listen for," "NVC in action," and "complex uses." The booklet is inexpensive; it's very portable, and I find it refreshing. (Reviewed by L. A. Mc Coy)

Marshall Rosenberg Live! (a transcript of three workshops with Marshall)

I love this book! I enjoy reading the question-response style of the transcribed interchanges between Marshall and participants in a workshop. It helps me understand the practice of NVC more deeply as I can go back over the discussion points slowly, quickly, once or often. I can read some of these passages to my children (ages 6 and 8) who find Marshall very funny—and they really get the meaning! It's like a workshop with Marshall right there in your hands, head, and heart whenever you want it. Marshall, I imagine, loves speaking and direct teaching much more than writing—this seems to meet both of our needs quite satisfactorily! (Reviewed by P. S. O'Grady)

NVC for Educators, aka *NVC: Language of the Heart*

In this approximately one hour audiotape of the National Center for Montessori Educators 1999 keynote presentation on Nonviolent Communication, Marshall presents his basic introduction to NVC. He talks about the four components: observation, feeling, need, and request, and the meaning of Giraffe and Jackal. The audience participates as Marshall leads them through the process, giving them Giraffe nods and Jackal howls. (This is NVC, however, so the howls—expressions of the Jackal's unmet needs—are more cuddly than ferocious.) An excellent, entertaining tape that makes a fine accompaniment to driving, cooking dinner, washing dishes, or changing the oil. (Reviewed by L. May)

Raising Children Compassionately: Parenting the Nonviolent Communication Way by Marshall B. Rosenberg, Ph.D.

The most important message I found in this small booklet is the power of unconditional love for children and the recognition that each person has the power to make healthy decisions. Our job as parents is not to make the decisions for our children as they grow, but to encourage and support them as they learn to understand and know themselves. The practice for me as a parent is to keep in mind every moment the autonomy of each of my children and encourage them to recognize their own feelings and needs. (Reviewed by E. Van Bronkhorst)

The Mayor of Jackal Heights by Rita Herzog and Kathy Smith

This wonderful story written for children can be an intriguing and empowering tale for those of any age. It is based on the premise that "scared and lonely" is the "almost always" feeling that Jackals are experiencing. With that insight, the Mayor, with the help of a Giraffe, is able to turn a miserable situation into one of harmony and peace. Lots of dialogue between the Giraffe and Jackal makes this a lively and realistic story. (Reviewed by M. Reed)

Marshall's Music 1 and 2 (audiotapes)

• *Marshall's Music 1*
Written by Marshall but performed mostly by an unidentified musician, these are folksongs with a political bent from the 70's. Done in a hillbilly bluesy style with clear lyrics, these songs provide satirical commentary on the many life-alienating messages woven through our culture.

• *Marshall's Music 2*
These gentle folksongs, all sung by Marshall, are delightful reminders of simple ways of being and inspire thoughtfulness in our everyday lives. The exception may be the "Titless Bitch Blues," which may be offensive to some listeners. Several of Marshall's workshop favorites are available here for those who would enjoy learning them to sing along. (Reviewed by M. Reed)

Making Life Wonderful (videotapes, Parts I and II out of a series of four)

In *Making Life Wonderful* (Parts I and II), Marshall Rosenberg reviews the basic steps of the Nonviolent Communication process. He takes on various roles in two full role-plays with workshop participants: one between a frustrated father and his reluctant-to-communicate teenage daughter, and the other between a woman and her estranged lover. Within these dialogues he skillfully weaves in many aspects of the NVC process. You will gain a deeper understanding of:
  —giving yourself empathy in a difficult dialogue
  —enjoying the Jackal show
  —limiting expressions to 40 words in order to keep the connection
  —the importance of taking your time
  —bringing yourself back to life

—using present requests to keep the flow going

—"enjoying" another's pain

—how to trust the energy working through human beings that can heal anything

—how not to blame, diagnose, analyze, fix, or interpret

—how "the story" (that we have been taught) gets in the way

—how most of our pain is created by images of what is actually happening

—how to respond to challenging reactions

—how to respond when a person doesn't hear what's in your heart

—how to avoid hearing what a Jackal thinks

—how to avoid reinforcing the belief that someone else is responsible for your feelings

—the ultimate test of "Giraffe ears"

—seeing needs as gifts

—empathizing with and keeping alive the implicit request to stay connected

—taking responsibility for your behavior without thinking you've caused another person's pain

—not hearing criticism as criticism

—mourning in Giraffe rather than apologizing

—why to avoid objectives that focus on getting rid of something (Reviewed by R. Rose)

Resolving Conflicts with Children and Adults (video)

This video presents Marshall Rosenberg doing some of what he does best. He combines clear explanations with a thought-provoking teaching style that inspires the listeners to come to their own understanding. Although questions from the audience are not audible on this tape, and I found some of the explanations to meander a bit, the video gives us a workshop strong on presenting a non-coercive, win-win paradigm. It also holds some of the typical Marshall Rosenberg wit and humor that I so enjoy. (Reviewed by A. Seid)

Notes

Clearly expressing how **I am** without blaming or criticizing	Empathically receiving how **you are** without hearing blame or criticism

OBSERVATIONS

1. What I observe *(see, hear, remember, imagine, free from my evaluations)* that does or does not contribute to my well-being:

   "When I (see, hear) . . . "

1. What you observe *(see, hear, remember, imagine, free from your evaluations)* that does or does not contribute to your well-being:

   "When you see/hear . . . "

   (Sometimes dropped when offering empathy)

FEELINGS

2. How I feel *(emotion or sensation rather than thought)* in relation to what I observe:

   "I feel . . . "

2. How you feel *(emotion or sensation rather than thought)* in relation to what you observe:

   "You feel . . ."

NEEDS

3. What I need or value *(rather than a preference, or a specific action)* that causes my feelings:

   " . . . because I need/value . . . "

3. What you need or value *(rather than a preference, or a specific action)* that causes your feelings:

   " . . . because you need/value . . ."

Clearly requesting that which would enrich **my** life without demanding	Empathically receiving that which would enrich **your** life without hearing any demand

REQUESTS

4. The concrete actions I would like taken:

   "Would you be willing to . . . ?"

4. The concrete actions you would like taken:

   "Would you like . . . ?"

   (Sometimes dropped when offering empathy)

Some Basic Feelings We All Have

Feelings when needs "are" fulfilled

- Amazed
- Confident
- Energetic
- Glad
- Inspired
- Joyous
- Optimistic
- Relieved
- Surprised
- Touched
- Comfortable
- Eager
- Fulfilled
- Hopeful
- Intrigued
- Moved
- Proud
- Stimulated
- Thankful
- Trustful

Feelings when needs "are not" fulfilled

- Angry
- Confused
- Disappointed
- Distressed
- Frustrated
- Hopeless
- Irritated
- Nervous
- Puzzled
- Sad
- Annoyed
- Concerned
- Discouraged
- Embarrassed
- Helpless
- Impatient
- Lonely
- Overwhelmed
- Reluctant
- Uncomfortable

Some Basic Needs We All Have

Autonomy

- Choosing dreams/goals/values
- Choosing plans for fulfilling one's dreams, goals, values

Celebration

- Celebrate the creation of life and dreams fulfilled
- Celebrate losses: loved ones, dreams, etc. (mourning)

Integrity

- Authenticity • Creativity
- Meaning • Self-worth

Interdependence

- Acceptance • Appreciation
- Closeness • Community
- Consideration
- Contribute to the enrichment of life
- Emotional Safety • Empathy

Physical Nurturance

- Air • Food
- Movement, exercise
- Protection from life-threatening forms of life: viruses, bacteria, insects, predatory animals
- Rest • Sexual expression
- Shelter • Touch • Water

Play

- Fun • Laughter

Spiritual Communion

- Beauty • Harmony
- Inspiration • Order • Peace

- Honesty (the empowering honesty that enables us to learn from our limitations)
- Love • Reassurance
- Respect • Support
- Trust • Understanding

About PuddleDancer Press

PuddleDancer Press (PDP) is the premier publisher of Nonviolent Communication™ related works. Its mission is to provide high quality materials that help people create a world in which all needs are met compassionately. PDP is the unofficial marketing arm of the international Center for Nonviolent Communication. Publishing revenues are used to develop and implement NVC promotion, educational materials and media campaigns. By working in partnership with CNVC, NVC trainers, teams and local supporters, PDP has created a comprehensive, cost-effective promotion effort that has helped bring NVC to thousands more people each year.

Since 2003, PDP has donated over 50,000 NVC books to organizations, decision-makers and individuals in need around the world. This program is supported in part by donations to CNVC, and by partnerships with like-minded organizations around the world. To ensure the continuation of this program, please make a tax-deductible donation to CNVC, earmarked to the Book Giveaway Campaign at www.CNVC.org/donation

Visit the PDP website at www.NonviolentCommunication.com to find the following resources:

- **Shop NVC** – Continue your learning—purchase our NVC titles online safely and conveniently. Find multiple-copy and package discounts, learn more about our authors and read dozens of book endorsements from renowned leaders, educators, relationship experts and more.

- **e-Newslette**r – Sign up today to stay apprised of new NVC titles, and to access expert articles, case studies and exclusive specials on NVC books, teleclasses and more with our free NVC Quick Connect e-Newsletter. Archived newsletters are also available.

- **Help Share NVC** – Access hundreds of valuable tools, resources and adaptable documents to help you share NVC, form a local NVC community, coordinate NVC workshops and trainings, and promote the life-enriching benefits of NVC training to organizations and communities in your area. Sign up for our NVC Promotion e-Bulletin to get all the latest tips and tools.

- **For the Press** – Journalists and producers can access author bios and photos, recently published articles in the media, video clips and other valuable information.

- **About NVC** – Learn more about these life-changing communication skills including an overview of the 4-part process, Key Facts About NVC, benefits of the NVC process, and access to our NVC e-Newsletter and Article Archives.

For more information, please contact PuddleDancer Press at:

P.O. Box 231129 • Encinitas CA 92024
Phone: 858-759-6963 • Fax: 858-759-6967
Email: email@puddledancer.com • www.NonviolentCommunication.com

About CNVC and NVC

About CNVC

Founded in 1984 by Dr. Marshall B. Rosenberg, The Center for Nonviolent Communication (CNVC) is an international nonprofit peacemaking organization whose vision is a world where everyone's needs are met peacefully. CNVC is devoted to supporting the spread of Nonviolent Communication (NVC) around the world.

Around the globe, training in NVC is now being taught in communities, schools, prisons, mediation centers, churches, businesses, professional conferences and more. Dr. Rosenberg spends more than 250 days each year teaching NVC in some of the most impoverished, war-torn states of the world. More than 200 certified trainers and hundreds more teach NVC in 35 countries to approximately 250,000 people each year.

At CNVC we believe that NVC training is a crucial step to continue building a compassionate, peaceful society. Your tax-deductible donation will help CNVC continue to provide training in some of the most impoverished, violent corners of the world. It will also support the development and continuation of organized projects aimed at bringing NVC training to high-need geographic regions and populations.

CNVC provides many valuable resources to support the continued growth of NVC worldwide. To make a tax-deductible donation or to learn more about the resources available, visit their website at **www.CNVC.org**.

For more information, please contact CNVC at:
2428 Foothill Blvd., Suite E • La Crescenta, CA 91214
Phone: 818-957-9393 • Fax: 818-957-1424
Email: cnvc@cnvc.org • www.cnvc.org

About NVC

From the bedroom to the boardroom, from the classroom to the war zone, Nonviolent Communication (NVC) is changing lives every day. NVC provides an easy to grasp, effective method to get to the root of violence and pain peacefully. By examining the unmet needs behind what we do or say, NVC helps reduce hostility, heal pain, and strengthen professional and personal relationships.

NVC helps us reach beneath the surface and discover what is alive and vital within us, and how all of our actions are based on human needs that we are seeking to meet. We learn to develop a vocabulary of feelings and needs that helps us more clearly express what is going on in us at any given moment. When we understand and acknowledge our needs, we develop a shared foundation for much more satisfying relationships. Join the thousands of people worldwide who have improved their relationships and their lives with this simple yet revolutionary process.

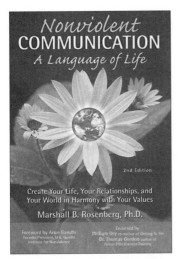

Nonviolent Communication:
A Language of Life, Second Edition

Create Your Life, Your Relationships and Your World in Harmony with Your Values

Marshall B. Rosenberg, Ph.D.

$17.95 — Trade Paper 6x9, 240pp
ISBN: 1-892005-03-4

Most of us are hungry for skills to improve the quality of our relationships, to deepen our sense of personal empowerment or to simply communicate more effectively. In this internationally acclaimed text, Marshall Rosenberg offers insightful stories, anecdotes, practical exercises and role-plays that will literally change your approach to communication for the better. Discover how the language you use can strengthen your relationships, build trust, prevent conflicts and heal pain. Revolutionary, yet simple, NVC offers the most effective tools to reduce violence and create peace — one interaction at a time.

Over 150,000 copies of this landmark book have been sold in 20 languages around the globe.

"Unless, as grandfather would say, 'we become the change we wish to see in the world,' no change will ever take place . . . If we change ourselves we can change the world, and changing ourselves begins with changing our language and methods of communication. I highly recommend reading this book and applying the Nonviolent Communication process it teaches."

> — **Foreword by Arun Gandhi**, *grandson of Mahatma Gandhi and co-founder of the AK Gandhi Institute for Nonviolence*

"Nonviolent communication is a simple yet powerful methodology for communicating in a way that meets both parties' needs. This is one of the most useful books you will ever read."

> — **William Ury**, co-author of *Getting to Yes* and author of *The Third Side*

"I believe the principles and techniques in this book can literally change the world, but more importantly, they can change the quality of your life with your spouse, your children, your neighbors, your coworkers and everyone else you interact with."

> — **Jack Canfield**, author, *Chicken Soup for the Soul*

Available from PDP, CNVC, all major bookstores, and Amazon.com
Distributed by IPG: 800-888-4741

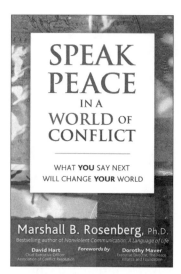

Speak Peace in a World of Conflict

What You Say Next Will Change the World

by Marshall B. Rosenberg, Ph.D.

$15.95 – Trade Paper 5-3/8x8-3/8, 240pp
ISBN: 1-892005-17-4

In every interaction, every conversation, and in every thought, you have a choice — to promote peace or perpetuate violence. International peacemaker, mediator, and healer, Dr. Marshall Rosenberg shows you how the language you use is the key to enriching life. Take the first step to reduce violence, heal pain, resolve conflicts and spread peace on our planet — by developing an internal consciousness of peace rooted in the language you use each day.

Speak Peace is filled with inspiring stories, lessons and ideas drawn from over 40 years of mediating conflicts and healing relationships in some of the most war torn, impoverished, and violent corners of the world. *Speak Peace* offers insight, practical skills, and powerful tools that will profoundly change your relationships and the course of your life for the better.

Bestselling author of the internationally acclaimed, *Nonviolent Communication: A Language of Life*

Discover how you can create an internal consciousness of peace as the first step toward effective personal, professional, and social change. Find complete chapters on the mechanics of Speaking Peace, conflict resolution, transforming business culture, transforming enemy images, addressing terrorism, transforming authoritarian structures, expressing and receiving gratitude, and social change.

"*Speak Peace* is a book that comes at an appropriate time when anger and violence dominates human attitudes. Marshall Rosenberg gives us the means to create peace through our speech and communication. A brilliant book.
— **Arun Gandhi, President**, *M. K. Gandhi Institute for Nonviolence, USA*

"*Speak Peace* sums up decades of healing and peacework. It would be hard to list all the kinds of people who can benefit from reading this book, because it's really any and all of us."

— **Dr. Michael Nagler**, author, *America Without Violence* and *Is There No Other Way: A Search for Nonviolent Future*

Available from PDP, CNVC, all major bookstores, and Amazon.com
Distributed by IPG: 800-888-4741

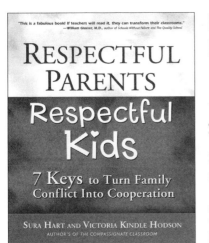

Trade Booklets from PuddleDancer Press

Being Me, Loving You • *A Practical Guide to Extraordinary Relationships* **by Marshall B. Rosenberg, Ph.D.** • Discover the "how-to" of heart to heart connections strengthened by joyfully giving and receiving. 80pp, ISBN: 1-892005-16-6 • **$6.95**

Getting Past the Pain Between Us • *Healing and Reconciliation Without Compromise* **by Marshall B. Rosenberg, Ph.D.** • Learn the healing power of listening and speaking from the heart. Skills for resolving conflicts, healing old hurts, and reconciling strained relationships. 48pp, ISBN: 1-892005-07-7 • **$6.95**

The Heart of Social Change • *How to Make a Difference in Your World* **by Marshall B. Rosenberg, Ph.D.** • Learn how creating an internal consciousness of compassion can impact your social change efforts. 48pp, ISBN: 1-892005-10-7 • **$6.95**

Parenting From Your Heart • *Sharing the Gifts of Compassion, Connection, and Choice* **by Inbal Kashtan** • Addresses the challenges of parenting with real-world solutions for creating family relationships that meet everyone's needs. 48pp, ISBN: 1-892005-08-5 • **$6.95**

Practical Spirituality • *Reflections on the Spiritual Basis of Nonviolent Communication* **by Marshall B. Rosenberg, Ph.D.** • Marshall's views on the spiritual origins and underpinnings of NVC, and how practicing the process helps him connect to the Divine. 48pp, ISBN: 1-892005-14-X • **$6.95**

Raising Children Compassionately • *Parenting the Nonviolent Communication Way* **by Marshall B. Rosenberg, Ph.D.** • Filled with insight and stories, this booklet will prove invaluable to parents, teachers, and others who want to nurture children and themselves. 32pp, ISBN: 1-892005-09-3 • **$5.95**

The Surprising Purpose of Anger • *Beyond Anger Management: Finding the Gift* **by Marshall B. Rosenberg, Ph.D.** • Learn the key truths about what anger is really telling us. Use it to uncover your needs and get them met in constructive ways. 48pp, ISBN: 1-892005-15-8 • **$6.95**

Teaching Children Compassionately • *How Students and Teachers Can Succeed with Mutual Understanding* **by Marshall B. Rosenberg, Ph.D.** • Skills for creating a successful classroom—from a keynote address and workshop given to a national conference of Montessori educators. 48pp, ISBN: 1-892005-11-5 • **$6.95**

We Can Work It Out • *Resolving Conflicts Peacefully and Powerfully* **by Marshall B. Rosenberg, Ph.D.** • Practical suggestions for fostering empathic connection, genuine cooperation, and satisfying resolutions in even the most difficult situations. 32pp, ISBN: 1-892005-12-3 • **$5.95**

What's Making You Angry? • *10 Steps to Transforming Anger So Everyone Wins* **by Shari Klein and Neill Gibson** • A step-by-step guide to re-focus your attention when you're angry, and create outcomes that are satisfying for everyone. 32pp, ISBN: 1-892005-13-1 • **$5.95**

Available from PDP, CNVC, all major bookstores and Amazon.com. Distributed by IPG: 800-888-4741. For more information about these booklets or to order online visit www.NonviolentCommunication.com

NVC Materials Available from CNVC

*Available from the Center for Nonviolent Communication
at www.CNVC.org or call 800-255-7696.*

The Giraffe Classroom **$18**
by Nancy Sokol Green • 8.5x11, 122pp, (spiral bound) • Humorous, creative, and thought provoking activities. Ideal for teachers, parents, and anyone who wants to use concrete exercises to learn the process of NVC.

Communication Basics **$4**
An Overview of Nonviolent Communication (24pp)
by Rachelle Lamb • This new booklet provides a clear, concise, and handy summary of what one might learn in an introductory training in Nonviolent Communication.

Nonviolent Communication **$10**
The Basics as I Know and Use Them (4x7, 94pp)
by Wayland Myers, Ph.D • A clear, compassionate, simple and practical presentation of NVC applied interpersonally.

The Basics of Nonviolent Communication **$50**
An Introductory Training (2 videotapes, 3hrs)
by Marshall B. Rosenberg, Ph.D. • This edited one-day training shows how we can connect with others in a way that enables everyone's needs to be met through natural giving.

Making Life Wonderful **$100**
An Intermediate Training (4 videotapes, over 8hrs)
by Marshall B. Rosenberg, Ph.D. • Improve relationships with self and others by increasing fluency in NVC. Two-day training session in San Francisco filled with insights, examples, extended role-plays, stories, and songs that will deepen your grasp of NVC.

THESE AND ADDITIONAL MATERIALS AVAILABLE AT:
(10% Member Discount available—Prices may change.)

Mail: CNVC, 2428 Foothill Blvd., Suite E, La Crescenta, CA 91214

Phone: 800-255-7696 (toll free order line) or by Fax: 1-818-957-1424

Shipping: Call 1-818-957-9393 to determine actual shipping charges.
Please pay with US dollars only.

Contributions and Membership: A contribution of $35 or more qualifies you as a member of CNVC and entitles you to a 10% discount on CNVC materials ordered from the Center. Your tax-deductible contribution of any amount will be gratefully received and will help support CNVC projects worldwide.

About Lucy Leu

Growing up bilingual and bicultural in Taiwan, Lucy Leu took an early interest in languages and the bridging of cultures. She began practicing Insight Meditation in 1986, and shortly thereafter her teaching career turned toward peace education. As a witness to the response of prisoners to Marshall Rosenberg's presentation of Nonviolent Communication (NVC), she was inspired to join the international Center for Nonviolent Communication as a trainer. Currently she serves on the Freedom Project, which supports the transition of prisoners into peacemakers to build safe communities founded on effective connections. Sharing with others the practices of NVC and mindfulness that have transformed her own life has left her feeling deeply rewarded. She is especially gratified to work side by side with colleagues who received NVC training inside prison and have since become peacemakers in their own communities. Lucy Leu is married, has two grown children, and is grateful for the opportunity she now has to tend to her elders.

Find out more about the Freedom Project at: Freedom_Project@hotmail.com